Will AI Kill Our Jobs?

By
Gowtham Periyasamy

About the Book

Will AI Kill Our Jobs?

Artificial Intelligence (AI) has rapidly entered the global workforce, transforming industries and sparking debates about its potential impact on jobs. The central question of this book, "Will AI Kill Our Jobs?" explores this topic from multiple perspectives, delving into both the fears and opportunities associated with the rise of intelligent machines.

The Fear of Job Loss

Throughout history, every technological revolution — from the Industrial Revolution to the rise of computers — has been accompanied by fears of mass job loss. This same fear surrounds AI today. Many worry that AI's ability to automate complex tasks could make entire professions obsolete. Jobs in fields like manufacturing, transportation, and data entry are often cited as vulnerable to automation. The rise of autonomous vehicles, machine learning algorithms, and intelligent robots that can perform tasks once thought exclusive to humans, such as diagnosing illnesses or analyzing large sets of data, amplifies concerns of widespread unemployment.

The book explores real-life scenarios where automation has led to job displacement. For example, autonomous vehicles

i

are already threatening to replace traditional driving jobs, and AI-powered customer service tools are reducing the need for human agents in call centers. The possibility of large-scale unemployment looms for workers in industries where routine, repetitive tasks are being automated by AI-driven systems.

The Opportunity for Job Transformation

However, the other side of the debate reveals a more optimistic perspective. Just as past technological advancements disrupted the workforce but also created new opportunities, AI presents the potential for job transformation rather than elimination. The key argument here is that while AI may take over certain tasks, it will also create new jobs, industries, and roles that do not yet exist.

The book highlights numerous examples where AI has not replaced human workers but empowered them to focus on higher-level, more fulfilling tasks. In industries like healthcare, AI is assisting doctors by quickly analyzing medical data, but it is the physicians who use these insights to make decisions, emphasizing the collaboration between human intuition and machine efficiency. Similarly, in manufacturing, robots handle repetitive, dangerous tasks, allowing workers to shift into roles as robot operators, technicians, and engineers, focusing on more creative and strategic responsibilities.

The Middle Ground: Humans and AI as Collaborators

The central theme of the book posits that the future of work lies in **collaboration** between humans and AI, not in competition. AI's strength lies in its ability to handle large-scale data processing, automate routine tasks, and optimize efficiency. However, human creativity, empathy, critical thinking, and emotional intelligence remain irreplaceable, ensuring that there are essential roles only people can fulfill.

For instance, while AI systems in education can personalize learning for students, it is still teachers who inspire, guide, and emotionally connect with learners. In hospitality, AI can streamline operations, but the personal touch of human service remains a vital part of the customer experience. AI systems excel at crunching numbers and processing data, but humans are needed to provide judgment, nuance, and moral considerations.

Adapting to the Future: Lifelong Learning and Reskilling

One of the book's key takeaways is the importance of **adaptability**. In a rapidly changing job market, workers must be prepared to continuously learn new skills. The book stresses the role of lifelong learning, reskilling, and upskilling to remain relevant in an AI-driven world. Industries and governments must invest in education and training programs to equip workers with the tools they need to thrive alongside AI.

New professions are already emerging as a result of AI's rise—roles like AI ethicists, automation engineers, and data scientists are in demand. The book suggests that workers who are willing to embrace change, adapt to new technologies, and learn how to work collaboratively with AI will find themselves in stronger positions in the future workforce.

The Ethical Challenge of AI

While the book outlines the benefits AI brings, it also addresses the challenges of training AI systems in the **right way**. If AI is poorly trained or biased, it can amplify inequality and create ethical concerns in the workplace. The book emphasizes the importance of developing AI systems that are fair, unbiased, and inclusive, ensuring that the benefits of AI are distributed equitably across society.

A Balanced Perspective

In the end, *Will AI Kill Our Jobs?* Does not offer a simple yes or no answer to the central question. Instead, it presents a nuanced perspective: AI will undoubtedly change the job landscape, and some jobs will disappear. However, it also opens up opportunities for new roles and empowers workers to collaborate with technology in ways that enhance productivity and creativity.

The book ultimately suggests that AI's impact on jobs depends largely on how businesses, governments, and workers respond to this change. By fostering a culture of adaptability, investing in education, and viewing AI as a tool for empowerment rather than replacement, the future of work can be one of collaboration between humans and intelligent machines—not a world where jobs are lost, but one where they are transformed.

Key Takeaways:

1. **AI as a Threat**: AI poses a real risk of displacing jobs, especially those reliant on repetitive, predictable tasks.
2. **AI as a Partner**: AI can augment human labor, allowing workers to focus on more complex, creative, and fulfilling tasks.
3. **Adaptability is Key**: Lifelong learning and upskilling are essential for workers to thrive in the evolving AI-driven job market.
4. **Collaboration, Not Competition**: The future of work lies in collaboration between humans and AI, utilizing the strengths of both to drive progress.
5. **Ethical Considerations**: Developing fair, unbiased AI systems is crucial for ensuring that the benefits of AI are shared by all.

AI won't kill jobs; it will **transform the future of work**—for those ready to adapt, learn, and grow alongside it.

Index

About the Book i

Introduction 1

The Dawn of Computing – Foundations of Technological Change 11

The Rise of Automation – A New Age of Intelligent Machines 19

AI in Everyday Life – How Intelligent Systems Are Changing Our World 27

Training tomorrow's AI – Building the Brains of the Future 37

Training AI the Right Way – Shaping the Future of Intelligent Machines 45

The Consequences of Misguided AI – What Happens When We Train AI the Wrong Way 53

Training AI for the Future World – Essentials for Building Tomorrow's Workforce 61

AI's Role in Revolutionizing Engineering, IT, Manufacturing, and Beyond 69

AI's Role in Revolutionizing Marketing, Customer Service, Healthcare, and Education 79

AI's Role in Finance, Human Resources, Agriculture, and Government 87

AI in Creative Fields, Hospitality, and Tourism – Redefining Human Expression 95

Will AI Kill Our Jobs? The Future of Work in a Machine-Driven World 107

AI and the Future of Work: Reinvention, Not Elimination 115

AI Energizes the Workforce: Amplifying Human Potential 117

Conclusion: The Future of Work – Humans and AI, Partners in Progress 124

Acknowledgment 131

Postscript 133

Introduction

"By 2023, over 40% of job postings in tech sectors mention AI-related skills — a sharp increase from just 15% five years ago. As AI continues to evolve, it's not a question of if it will change our work, but how quickly and to what extent".

Whether you're a factory worker, teacher, or financial analyst, the question on everyone's mind is the same: how will AI impact my job?

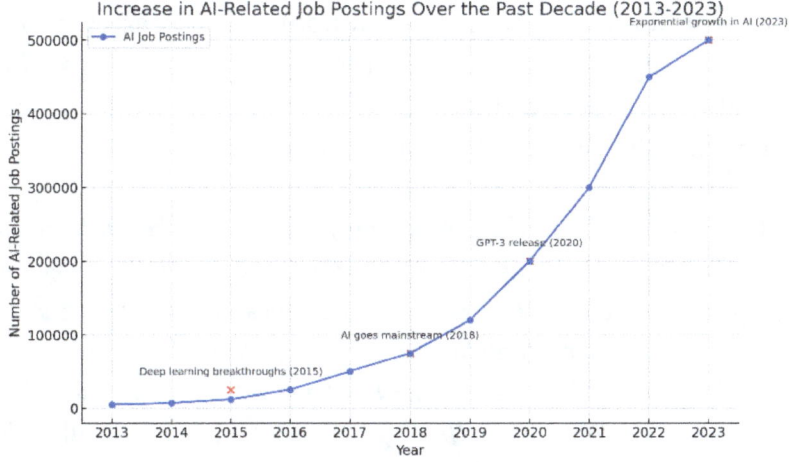

Increase in AI-Related Job Postings over the Past Decade (2013-2023)

Introduction

Will AI Kill Our Jobs?

"It was a routine shift for Sarah, a nurse at one of the busiest hospitals in Chicago. Like many of her colleagues, she was used to the fast pace of the emergency room – triaging patients, organizing data, and making quick decisions. But today, she noticed something unusual. A new tool had arrived: an AI-powered diagnostic system. It could analyze patient symptoms and recommend possible treatments in seconds. At first, Sarah feared it would replace her. But over the next few months, something remarkable happened – Sarah found that the AI allowed her to spend more time with her patients, focusing on what really mattered: the human connection that no machine could ever replace."

Across industries, similar stories are unfolding. AI is entering the workforce – analyzing data, automating processes, and, in some cases, even making decisions. For every person like Sarah, who found that AI enhanced her work, there's someone else with a different experience.

"On the other side of the world, Amit, a factory worker in Mumbai, watched as a robotic arm moved methodically through the factory floor, doing the work he had done for the past decade. The machine was tireless, never taking breaks, and it was faster than any human could ever be. Within months, Amit's job was gone, replaced by a machine. The promise of technology had delivered a hard truth – his skills were no longer needed."

"David, a seasoned taxi driver in Phoenix, Arizona, was watching the rise of Waymo's self-driving cars with growing concern. He had

spent years driving through the city streets, taking pride in his local knowledge and the relationships he built with regular passengers. But as autonomous vehicles began to increase in numbers, David's worries turned to reality: fewer passengers needed a human driver. Eventually, his job disappeared. Faced with a career crossroads, David took a leap of faith. He retrained, transitioning from driving to a new role as a fleet technician for Waymo's self-driving cars. Now, instead of fighting against the AI-driven future, David is part of it, ensuring that the cars stay on the road safely. 'I never thought I'd be working alongside the very machines that replaced me,' David reflects. 'But this isn't the end. It's just a new chapter.'"

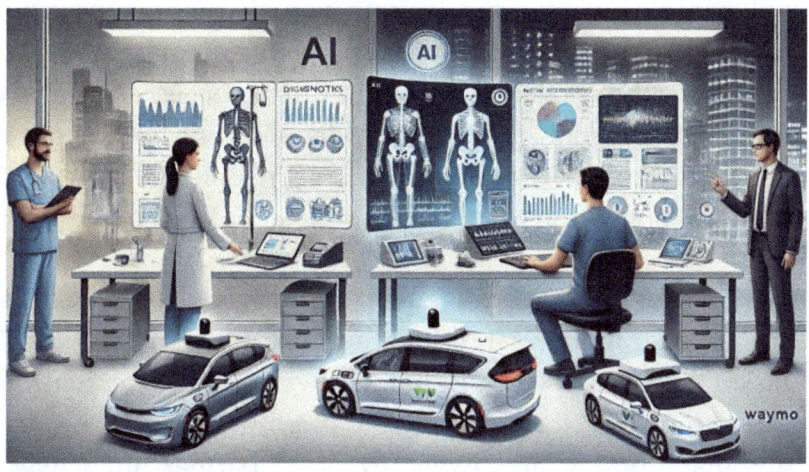

Sarah working with AI in healthcare & David transitioning into AI-powered transportation with Waymo

These contrasting stories bring to life the central question of this book: *Will AI kill our jobs?*

Introduction

The Fear Factor: Fiction vs. Reality

For decades, popular culture has fed our deepest fears about technology. In dystopian films like *The Terminator* and *I, Robot*, machines take over every aspect of life, rendering humans obsolete or even threatening their survival. In these exaggerated futures, AI-driven robots control everything—from manufacturing to governing societies—leaving humans powerless.

These fictional scenarios play on a primal fear: that machines will become too powerful, leaving no room for human agency or creativity. While these dystopian visions may seem like distant science fiction, they tap into real concerns about the rise of automation and AI in today's world. However, in reality, AI's greatest potential lies in collaboration with humans, not in domination or complete replacement.

While AI is often portrayed as the ultimate disruptor, the reality is far more nuanced. Rather than fully automating all tasks, AI is set to work in tandem with humans, enhancing our capabilities through collaboration. Instead of complete automation, AI is more likely to create a partnership between humans and machines, with AI handling repetitive, data-heavy tasks, and humans providing critical thinking, creativity, and empathy—qualities that machines cannot replicate.

The Age-Old Fear of Technology

Though exaggerated, these dystopian fears are rooted in a long-standing human anxiety — one that has surfaced with each technological revolution, threatening to disrupt the status quo. From the Industrial Revolution to the rise of computers, people have always asked the same question: Will this new technology make me obsolete?

Technological innovation has always come with anxiety. Whether it was the Luddites smashing textile machines during the Industrial Revolution, or clerks fearing the arrival of computers in the mid-20th century, each new era brings the same question: Will this new technology render me obsolete?

Today, artificial intelligence is the latest frontier in this long history of disruption. But unlike past technological revolutions, AI has the potential to replace not only manual labour but also cognitive tasks — those jobs we believed only humans could do. Yet, as history shows, technology doesn't just displace; it also creates new opportunities. Can AI follow this same pattern, or is it fundamentally different this time?

Real-Life Examples of AI at Work

Across the globe, we're already seeing the profound ways AI is reshaping work, and they look nothing like the dystopian futures Hollywood would have us imagine.

Introduction

AI plays a dual role: it automates repetitive tasks, freeing workers like Jon to focus on more creative and strategic decisions. Simultaneously, it empowers individuals like Aisha, offering insights and opportunities that were once out of reach. This dual role—enhancing human capabilities while automating routine processes—will define the future of work. While fears of job displacement are valid, these examples show that AI can augment human work rather than replace it, opening new doors for innovation and creativity.

"In Silicon Valley, Jon, a data analyst at a major tech company, realized something striking: his job was getting easier. A new AI tool had been implemented to analyse massive datasets that used to take him days to sort through manually. Now, it took mere hours. Rather than fearing for his position, Jon found that this freed him to focus on higher-level tasks, like developing strategies and making critical decisions that only a human could make. The AI did the heavy lifting, but Jon provided the judgment and context."

"Meanwhile, in a rural town in Kenya, Aisha, a farmer, noticed that her crop yields were improving. This was no accident. A new AI-driven app on her smartphone was analysing weather patterns, soil data, and market trends to recommend the best time to plant and harvest her crops. What once took generations of agricultural experience, Aisha could now access in real time, allowing her to make smarter decisions and provide for her family like never before."

These examples highlight AI's dual nature: freeing skilled workers like Jon to focus on strategic and creative decisions while empowering individuals like Aisha by offering advanced insights that were once only available to a select few.

What This Book Will Explore

In the following chapters, we will dive deep into the real-world impact of AI, answering the central question: Will AI kill our jobs? We will explore:

- **Industries on the cutting edge of AI** — from healthcare, where AI is accelerating diagnoses, to retail, where robotics and automation are transforming supply chains.
- **Historical parallels** — how past technologies, from the steam engine to the personal computer, were met with fear but ultimately led to new industries and job growth.
- **New opportunities created by AI** — how roles in data science, AI ethics, and **machine learning*** are flourishing as AI technology grows.
- **The importance of reskilling and lifelong learning** — why workers need to adapt to this new era, and how they can ensure they remain relevant in an AI-driven world.
- **Ethical challenges** — how we must ensure that AI development is fair, unbiased, and benefits all of humanity, not just a privileged few.

***Machine learning**, a branch of AI, is like teaching a computer how to recognize patterns by feeding it large amounts of data. Think of it *as training a dog to fetch, but instead of a stick, the AI is fetching relevant patterns from the data it has learned from.*

A New Future: Human-AI Collaboration

While the fears surrounding AI are valid, there is another side to the story. For every worker displaced by automation, there are new roles being created. This book will explore how AI can serve as a partner—augmenting human capabilities rather than replacing them.

"In Texas, James, a middle school teacher, began using an AI-powered educational platform that tailored lessons to each student's learning style and pace. For the first time, James saw his struggling students thrive, while his gifted students were more challenged. The AI tool gave him insights into his students' progress, allowing him to focus on teaching rather than administrative tasks. 'It hasn't replaced me,' James said. 'It's freed me to be a better teacher.'"

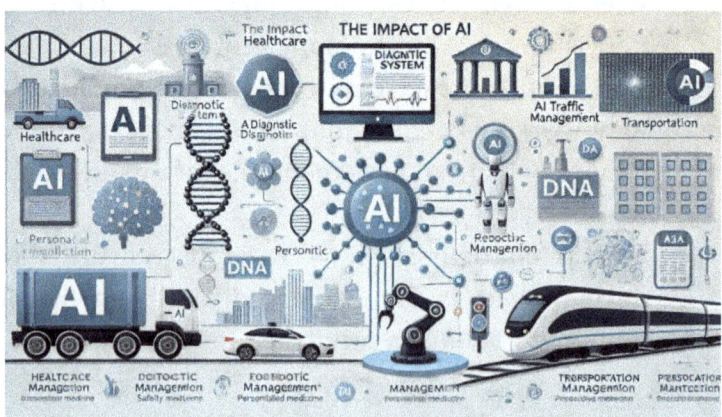

The Role of AI in Transforming Healthcare and Transportation

As we move forward, AI will undoubtedly take over certain tasks, but it is up to us to reshape the future of work.

Those who can adapt, innovate, and collaborate with AI will not only survive, but thrive. The key is to embrace AI as a powerful tool that, when guided by human intelligence, can create a more productive and innovative future.

Why This Book Matters

You're likely reading this book because you're wondering how AI will impact your career, industry, or future. Will your job be safe? Will you need to reskill to remain competitive?

In the chapters ahead, you'll find not only answers to these pressing questions, but also actionable strategies to help you thrive in this rapidly changing landscape.

Call to Action

Whether you're a factory worker worried about automation, a healthcare professional adapting to AI-driven diagnostics, an educator exploring AI-powered teaching tools, a business leader navigating digital transformation, or simply someone curious about the future of AI — this book is for you.

In a rapidly evolving world, adapting to AI is no longer optional — it's essential. Together, we'll explore how you can prepare for the future of work, ensuring that you don't just stay relevant but thrive and stay ahead of the curve in an AI-driven world.

The story of AI's impact on jobs isn't as simple as doom or deliverance. Let's take a closer look at how we got here, and what lies ahead.

The Dawn of Computing – Foundations of Technological Change

A World before Computers

Imagine living in a world where every financial forecast, astronomical observation, and statistical calculation was done entirely by hand. In the early 20th century, human "computers" performed complex calculations with nothing but pencils, paper, and sheer focus. These were often women, hunched over desks in cramped rooms, calculating for hours on end. This was the reality—a time when the need for precision was growing, but the tools to meet that need were still extremely limited.

But could human brains alone keep up with the world's growing complexity?

Take, for instance, the human "computers" who worked tirelessly during World War II, calculating missile trajectories. Often working through the night, the pressure was immense, and errors were frequent. These unsung heroes of warfare logistics used laborious methods, but the complexity of the problems they were solving was outpacing their abilities. Something more efficient, more powerful, was needed.

This pressure to innovate set the stage for the dawn of machines—ushering in a revolution that would forever change how we work.

Enter the Machines: The First Computers

In the 1940s, the world finally received a solution: massive, room-sized machines like ENIAC (Electronic Numerical Integrator and Computer). These early computers performed calculations at unimaginable speeds compared to a human. To give perspective: calculations that took a human hours could be completed by ENIAC in mere seconds.

Initially, these machines were built for military use. But soon, the potential to transform industries beyond the battlefield became impossible to ignore. Banks, insurance companies, and manufacturers saw the possibilities. People, however, were left wondering: Would these machines replace workers? Or could they bring about something far more unexpected?

The Banking Industry: Transforming, Not Replacing Jobs

In the 1960s, Barclays Bank in London introduced the world's first automated teller machine (ATM). At the time, widespread concern gripped bank tellers who feared this new machine would render their roles obsolete. Could a single machine replace their entire profession?

Yet, what happened was nothing short of surprising. Rather than eliminating the need for tellers, ATMs allowed banks to expand. By handling routine tasks like withdrawals and deposits, tellers were freed to focus on complex, higher-value tasks like financial planning and customer service. Not only did the number of bank branches increase, but employment in the sector grew.

ATMs didn't eliminate jobs—they transformed them, empowering workers to take on more meaningful roles. This early sign of transformation, rather than destruction, set a precedent for how technology might augment human work in the future.

But was this an anomaly, or a glimpse of a larger trend?

Fears of Obsolescence: The Rise of Automation Anxiety

As computing power continued to grow, so did the fear of widespread job loss. Workers in industries reliant on repetitive tasks—like data entry clerks and switchboard operators—were right to feel anxious. These machines could handle calculations, store vast amounts of data, and retrieve information faster than any human ever could. By the 1960s and '70s, entire departments of typists began to disappear as machines proved quicker and more accurate.

The fear was tangible. But what if technology didn't just replace roles — what if it created new ones?

From Typists to Tech Experts: Adaptation Amidst Automation

Take Mary, for example. In the early 1970s, she worked as a typist, transcribing documents on a manual typewriter. When word processors were introduced, Mary and her colleagues feared the worst. The machines could type faster, make fewer mistakes, and didn't require rest. Panic set in.

But instead of resisting the inevitable, Mary embraced it. She retrained to become a word processor operator, and over time, she transitioned into office management. Soon, Mary found herself managing teams using computerized systems, her career not just saved but transformed.

Mary's story speaks to the resilience and adaptability of the human spirit — a reminder that with each wave of new technology, opportunities arise for those willing to adapt. Could the same hold true for the technologies of today and tomorrow?

The IBM Revolution: Creating Jobs, Not Eliminating Them

IBM's introduction of mainframe computers in the 1950s — such as the IBM 701 — didn't just revolutionize industries; it created entire fields. These machines became the backbone of operations for businesses, but rather than decimating jobs, they did the opposite. IBM's innovations led to a demand for skilled operators, programmers, and technicians to maintain and run these computers.

This rise in demand gave birth to the IT industry, employing millions worldwide. IBM's advances demonstrated that rather than replacing human workers, technology could coexist and even thrive alongside them.

But as computers became smaller and more powerful, would the balance between humans and machines remain?

NASA and the Apollo Mission: Collaboration at Its Peak

One of the most iconic examples of human-machine collaboration came with NASA's Apollo moon landing in 1969. Computers were crucial for calculating the complex trajectories required to send astronauts to the Moon. But even with powerful machines, human ingenuity was indispensable.

Margaret Hamilton, a pioneering software engineer, developed the code for the Apollo guidance system. When errors occurred mid-flight, it was Hamilton's code, combined with the astronauts' quick thinking, that ensured the mission's success.

Computers didn't replace human effort—they enhanced it. Could this combination of human intellect and machine power help us achieve even greater things in the future?

The Impact on Productivity: How PCs Transformed the Office

By the 1980s, personal computers (PCs) were starting to become a common sight in offices. No longer confined to massive rooms, computers now fit neatly on desks, ready to streamline processes across industries. From law firms to hospitals, PCs began revolutionizing productivity, helping employees work faster and smarter.

The possibilities were endless—how else could these small, powerful machines reshape our daily work lives?

Microsoft and the Rise of Office Work: Empowering Workers

When Microsoft introduced its Office suite in the mid-1980s, it fundamentally changed how people worked. Tasks that once took days—like compiling financial reports—could now be done in hours using Excel. Far from causing job losses, PCs became essential tools that allowed employees to focus on more strategic, creative, and interpersonal aspects of their roles.

For example, financial analysts who had once spent hours manually crunching numbers now had the time to interpret data and offer deeper insights. Rather than replacing them, PCs empowered workers to do their jobs better and faster.

But as technology continued to evolve, one question persisted: *Could humans and machines reach even greater heights together?*

The Shift from Fear to Collaboration: A New Era

As computers grew more powerful, the initial fears of job loss began to wane. Over time, people realized that technology could be a powerful collaborator, not a threat. The key was learning how to work alongside these machines, not against them.

Could this mindset of collaboration be the key to thriving in the age of AI?

Automation in Manufacturing: Evolution, Not Extinction

In the 1990s, companies like Ford and General Motors introduced robotics into their assembly lines, sparking fears that human workers would be replaced. However, rather than making jobs obsolete, these robots created new roles. Workers who once manually assembled car parts became robot operators, engineers, and technicians, overseeing the automated processes.

This shift resulted in a more efficient production process and created higher-paying roles in robotics and engineering. Could this model of human-machine collaboration serve as a blueprint for the AI-driven workforce of the future?

The Lesson: Technology as a Partner, Not a Threat

The history of computing offers a crucial lesson: while technology may change the nature of work, it rarely eliminates jobs outright. Instead, it shifts our focus, creating new opportunities for those who adapt. Time and again, workers who embrace these changes, learn new skills, and collaborate with machines find themselves not just surviving but thriving.

From ATMs to personal computers, each leap in technology has offered new possibilities for workers. Far from being replaced, those who embrace the change often find new paths forward, as industries grow and evolve. As we enter the AI era, could this historical pattern hold true once again? Will AI empower us, just as previous technological revolutions have?

The Rise of Automation – A New Age of Intelligent Machines

The Automation Revolution

Imagine walking into a factory in the early 1900s. Men and women hunch over complex machines, manually assembling products, carefully stitching together the fabric of industrial progress. Fast-forward to today, and the factory floor looks drastically different. The once tireless human hands are now replaced with precision robots, handling the same tasks at a speed and accuracy unimaginable just decades ago. But this isn't the end of human labor—far from it.

Automation is no longer just about machines doing repetitive tasks. We're entering a new era, where artificial intelligence (AI) is stepping in, not to replace humans, but to work *with* them. It's no longer just robots on the assembly line—it's AI systems that can learn, adapt, and even make decisions.

But is this just the beginning? Could the next wave of AI-powered automation reshape work in ways we've never seen before?

Early Examples of Automation in Industries

Automation didn't just appear overnight—it evolved. To understand the present, we need to revisit the past. The early examples of automation were mechanical, focusing on boosting efficiency in industries like manufacturing.

Take the car industry, for example. In the 1990s, car manufacturers like Ford and General Motors introduced robotics to their assembly lines. These early robots didn't think for themselves—they followed pre-programmed instructions, performing repetitive tasks with precision and speed. They helped reduce errors, increase output, and prevent workplace injuries. However, they lacked intelligence—they couldn't learn, adapt, or improve themselves.

But what's fascinating is that this early wave of automation didn't eliminate jobs. Instead, it changed them. Workers who once assembled cars by hand became robot operators and technicians. The question now is: Could the same pattern apply to the next wave of automation, powered by AI?

As we step into this AI-driven age, the very nature of automation is transforming.

AI-Powered Automation: A New Frontier

Now, let's leap forward to the present day. The machines on the factory floor are no longer just following instructions—they're **thinking**. AI-powered systems don't just repeat the same tasks; they learn from their experiences. This marks the dawn of a new frontier: intelligent automation.

Picture an Amazon warehouse. Instead of workers walking miles every day to pick items, AI directs fleets of robots, analysing real-time data to ensure packages are picked, packed, and shipped faster than ever before. These robots communicate with each other, learn the most efficient paths, and even predict what items need to be restocked — tasks that would have taken dozens of human workers hours to accomplish.

But the story doesn't stop here. AI isn't just revolutionizing logistics; it's creeping into nearly every industry, reshaping the way we work and live. From the warehouse floor to the doctor's office, AI is transforming the world in ways that were once science fiction.

It's worth asking: *What does this AI automation mean for us?*

How Automation is Redefining Work Today

AI-powered automation is not just reserved for factory floors and warehouses. It's everywhere — from hospitals to retail stores, from finance to transportation. But don't take my word for it — let's look at some real-world examples.

In **healthcare**, robots are now assisting surgeons in the operating room. Systems like the Da Vinci robotic surgery platform allow doctors to perform intricate surgeries with greater precision than ever before. But these robots don't act alone—they work under the guidance of skilled surgeons. This proves that even in this hyper-automated world, human expertise is still irreplaceable.

Retail is another industry that's seeing sweeping changes. Have you ever walked into an Amazon Go store? No cashiers, no lines—just AI-powered systems tracking what you pick up and ensuring you're automatically billed as you leave. Meanwhile, AI chatbots handle customer service inquiries, freeing up human employees to focus on more complex tasks.

Finance has seen a similar transformation. Complex trading algorithms now make split-second decisions based on millions of data points, performing tasks that once required entire teams of analysts. But again, humans play an essential role in overseeing and guiding these systems.

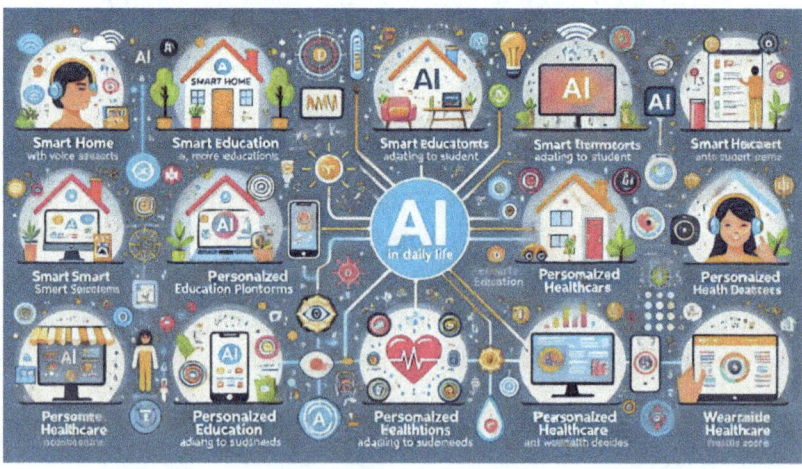

AI Integration in Everyday Domains

And then, there's the rise of **self-driving cars**. Companies like Waymo are pushing the envelope, developing vehicles that could eventually take over our daily commutes. But *what happens to the drivers whose livelihoods depend on driving? How do we navigate this new reality?*

The answers lie in understanding the pattern we've seen before—and the fears that arise with every technological shift.

Fears of Job Loss: Are We Repeating History?

Every technological revolution brings with it waves of anxiety. The rise of computers caused widespread fear among clerical workers. The rise of automation sparked concern among factory workers. And now, AI is triggering the same alarms. Are we simply repeating history?

In places like the **Rust Belt** in the U.S., the decline of traditional manufacturing led to economic hardship as automation took over. It's understandable why there's fear. When jobs disappear, the immediate instinct is to think the worst. But is this fear justified?

History tells us that while some jobs are indeed at risk, new ones often emerge to replace them. It happened during the Industrial Revolution, it happened with the rise of computers, and it could happen again.

So, are we on the verge of a mass unemployment crisis, or could the story of automation today be more nuanced?

Jobs at Risk vs. Jobs Being Created

As AI becomes more capable, it's natural to wonder: Which jobs are at risk? Will AI wipe out entire industries, or will it create new opportunities?

The truth is, some jobs will likely disappear. Repetitive, mundane tasks are prime candidates for automation. But here's the catch: while certain roles may be phased out, **new, more exciting ones are being created**. Think about it—20 years ago, no one had heard of data scientists, AI engineers, or automation consultants. Today, these roles are among the most in-demand careers globally.

Take the rise of **AI ethicists**, for example. As AI systems become more ingrained in our society, the need for experts to ensure they operate fairly, ethically, and without bias is growing. These are jobs that didn't exist before but are crucial to the future of AI.

Roles like 'AI ethicist' and 'automation engineer' are becoming essential as industries try to ensure their AI systems remain transparent and effective.

The lesson here is clear: while automation may change the job landscape, it also opens doors to opportunities we can't yet imagine.

But how do we ensure that humans continue to work with machines rather than be replaced by them?

Collaborating with Machines: The Future of Work

The future of work isn't about machines replacing humans — it's about machines and humans working together. AI is powerful, but it still lacks critical elements of human intelligence: creativity, empathy, and intuition.

Take the healthcare industry again. IBM's **Watson Health** can process vast amounts of data in seconds, making diagnostic suggestions for doctors. However, it's still up to the doctor to interpret the results, engage with the patient, and make the final decisions. It's a partnership, not a replacement.

Similarly, in fields like **marketing** or **design**, AI tools help generate ideas, analyse trends, and streamline workflows. But it's still the human touch that adds the creative spark or emotional resonance needed for success.

So, what does this partnership between humans and machines look like in practice? And more importantly, how can workers prepare for this future?

Preparing for the Future: Upskilling and Lifelong Learning

The key to thriving in an AI-driven world is **adaptability**. As AI continues to evolve, workers must embrace lifelong learning to stay competitive. This means constantly updating skills, whether through formal education, online courses, or on-the-job training.

Companies like **Google** and **Tesla** understand this. Google offers AI certifications that provide workers with the knowledge they need to navigate an AI-driven economy, while Tesla invests heavily in retraining programs for factory workers displaced by automation. These companies are showing us the way forward: embrace change, don't fear it.

But it's not just up to companies. What about governments and educational institutions? How can they play a role in preparing the workforce for an AI-driven future?

AI tools like IBM's Watson assist doctors by analysing complex medical data in seconds, but it's the doctors who interpret this data and apply human judgment to make life-saving decisions.

AI in Everyday Life – How Intelligent Systems Are Changing Our World

The Automation Revolution: AI's Quiet Takeover

It's 7:00 AM, and your alarm rings. But it's not just any alarm. This is a smart alarm, one that knows you've had a restless night and waits until the last possible moment to wake you up, ensuring you get every precious minute of sleep. As you rise, your smart thermostat has already adjusted the temperature to your ideal morning setting, and in the kitchen, the coffee machine hums to life, brewing your favourite blend — timed perfectly to greet you as you walk in.

Welcome to the world of AI — an era where machines quietly work in the background, anticipating your needs before you even have to ask.

Artificial intelligence, once confined to the imaginations of science fiction writers, is now a seamless part of our daily routines. From managing household tasks to guiding our conversations, AI has become a subtle, ever-present partner in modern life.

But how did we get here? How did AI move from concept to reality so quietly, and so thoroughly, that many of us didn't even notice the shift?

AI in the Home: A New Kind of Helper

Imagine returning home after a long day. As you approach your front door, facial recognition software unlocks it, and the lights in your living room flicker on to greet you. Your favourite music starts playing softly in the background, and the thermostat adjusts to the perfect temperature. This isn't some futuristic dream—it's a reality for millions of people across the world.

Smart home assistants like Amazon Alexa, Google Assistant, and Apple's Siri have become a fixture in households. These AI-powered devices have evolved from simple voice-activated search tools to comprehensive systems that manage everything from lighting and home security to grocery shopping and entertainment. The AI in your smart speaker knows when you usually wake up, what your daily schedule looks like, and how you like your coffee.

But the rise of AI in the home isn't just about convenience—it's about creating an interconnected ecosystem of devices that learn from your behaviour. Take smart appliances, for example. AI-powered vacuums map your home's layout, learning which areas need more attention and when to clean. Smart thermostats track your movements, adjusting the temperature throughout the day to save energy and reduce costs.

As we hand over more control to these intelligent systems, a question lingers:

Will AI Kill Our Jobs?

How much of our lives are we willing to automate, and where does convenience begin to blur into control?

AI in Communication: The Silent Assistant

When you text someone, have you ever noticed your phone's suggestions for what you might say next? That's AI in action. Whether it's predictive text, grammar correction, or even the filters on your social media posts, AI is quietly working behind the scenes to make communication faster, easier, and more personalized.

Diagram of AI-Powered Autonomous Systems

Take Google Translate, for instance. Traveling to a foreign country used to require either fluency in the local language or reliance on a phrasebook. Today, with AI-powered apps, you can translate conversations in real time. Not only does it

29

convert words, but it learns from user input, gradually improving its accuracy with each interaction.

Beyond translation, AI systems like Grammarly analyse the tone and structure of your writing, offering suggestions that not only correct mistakes but also enhance clarity and impact. This ability to refine our communication has become essential, especially in a world where messaging and written content are king.

But as AI improves how we communicate, it raises a fascinating question—could we reach a point where machines understand language better than we do, subtly shaping our thoughts and the way we interact with one another?

AI in Entertainment: Curating Your World

After a long day, you sit down on your couch, open Netflix, and immediately see a line-up of shows and movies curated just for you. The suggestions aren't random—they're carefully tailored by AI based on your past viewing habits. AI has become the quiet curator of our entertainment lives, crafting personalized experiences that make content consumption seamless.

In music, AI does more than just play songs. Platforms like Spotify analyse your listening history, track what songs you skip, and predict which new releases you'll like based on data from millions of users. Every playlist it suggests, every song it plays—it's all calculated to cater to your tastes.

In video gaming, AI takes this one step further. Procedural generation technology, as seen in games like *No Man's Sky*, creates entire virtual worlds from scratch, providing each player with a unique experience. The AI doesn't just generate random landscapes; it builds cohesive, expansive universes based on learned preferences and player behaviours.

With AI driving so much of what we watch, listen to, and play, the question becomes — *are we still choosing our entertainment, or is AI guiding our tastes in ways we don't fully realize?*

AI in Transportation: A Journey Toward Autonomy

Imagine stepping into your car, telling it where to go, and then sitting back as it navigates traffic, follows road signs, and ensures you arrive at your destination safely — all without you lifting a finger. Self-driving cars, once a far-off fantasy, are inching closer to reality, and AI is at the heart of this transformation.

Companies like Tesla, Waymo, and Uber are developing AI-powered autonomous vehicles that can interpret road conditions, anticipate hazards, and even learn from the behaviour of other drivers. These cars don't just drive — they make decisions, adapt to new environments, and improve their performance over time.

But even before fully autonomous vehicles hit the road, AI has already transformed how we navigate. Apps like Google Maps use real-time traffic data and AI algorithms to find the fastest routes, suggest detours, and even predict traffic patterns based on historical data.

As AI takes control of the wheel, it's worth asking — *what will happen to those whose livelihoods depend on driving? And are we ready to entrust our safety to intelligent machines?*

AI in Healthcare: A Digital Doctor in Your Pocket

AI's most life-changing contributions may lie in healthcare. Imagine being diagnosed with a disease in its earliest stages — before symptoms even appear — thanks to AI's ability to analyse vast amounts of data in seconds. In the realm of medicine, AI is already making waves.

Consider IBM's Watson, an AI that can sift through millions of medical records to assist doctors in diagnosing patients more accurately. By analysing medical images and data, AI can detect patterns that humans might miss. In some cases, AI systems have even outperformed doctors in diagnosing certain conditions, such as early-stage cancers.

Beyond diagnosis, AI-powered robots like the Da Vinci system assist surgeons in performing intricate surgeries with unprecedented precision. These robots don't replace the doctors — they enhance their skills, making procedures less invasive and reducing recovery times for patients.

Wearable devices powered by AI, like fitness trackers and smartwatches, are also revolutionizing personal healthcare. These devices continuously monitor heart rates, sleep patterns, and physical activity, offering personalized health advice and even alerting users to potential medical issues in real time.

As AI becomes more integral to healthcare, we must consider—*will there come a day when AI not only diagnoses but also treats patients independently?*

AI in Education: A Personalized Learning Experience

Picture this: You're sitting in a classroom, but instead of following a rigid, one-size-fits-all curriculum, every lesson is tailored specifically for you. AI is quietly revolutionizing education, making personalized learning not just a possibility but a reality.

AI-powered learning platforms like Duolingo and Coursera are using algorithms to track students' progress, adjust difficulty levels, and provide personalized feedback. Traditional classrooms are also adopting AI tools to assess student performance, allowing teachers to customize lesson plans based on individual needs.

The result? A more engaging, efficient, and personalized learning experience for students of all ages.

But what happens when AI plays a bigger role in the classroom—*could it one day replace teachers altogether? And if it does, what might education look like in the future?*

Privacy Concerns: The Cost of Convenience?

While AI makes our lives easier, it comes at a cost—our data. Every interaction we have with AI systems, from asking Siri a question to streaming a movie on Netflix, generates data. This data is collected, analysed, and used to make the AI smarter. But where does it go? And who's using it?

In an age where our phones track our locations, our smart assistants record our voices, and our browsing habits are analysed, privacy concerns are growing. Tech giants like Google and Facebook use AI to offer personalized services, but they also collect vast amounts of information about our lives.

As AI continues to grow more pervasive, we must ask ourselves—*how much of our personal privacy are we willing to trade for convenience? And who will safeguard our data in this AI-driven world?*

AI and Human Relationships: A New Kind of Bond

Beyond convenience, AI is starting to touch the most personal aspects of our lives—our relationships. Dating apps like Tinder use AI algorithms to suggest potential matches, while AI companions like Replika are designed to provide emotional support.

As AI continues to evolve, the lines between human and machine relationships may blur. Could we one day form deep, emotional bonds with AI companions? And if so, how will this change the nature of human connection?

As AI begins to influence our personal relationships, we must wonder—*will AI become a substitute for real human interaction, or can it enhance the way we connect?*

The Future of Everyday AI

AI has already transformed many aspects of our lives, often in ways we don't even notice. From the mundane tasks of managing our homes to the healthcare potential of AI in healthcare, intelligent systems have become part of the very fabric of modern society.

But as AI continues to grow more intelligent and integrated, the question is not how far it will go—but whether we're prepared for the future it brings. Will we guide AI, or will AI end up guiding us?

Training Tomorrow's AI – Building the Brains of the Future

The Foundation of AI: Data as the New Oil

Imagine sitting in front of your favourite music app, like Spotify. You press play, and somehow, the playlist feels tailor-made for you, reflecting your exact mood. How does this happen? Each time you choose a song, skip a track, or save a playlist, you're feeding an AI system, training it to learn your preferences. But what if, instead of music, this system was helping doctors make critical decisions in surgery or financial analysts predict market trends? Suddenly, the stakes feel much higher.

This is the power of data in AI. It's not just a tool for convenience—it's shaping the very world we live in. But as the saying goes, "garbage in, garbage out." If AI is trained on flawed, biased, or incomplete data, the consequences can ripple through entire industries.

But what happens when AI is trained correctly? Could it revolutionize the way we solve complex global problems?

The Importance of High-Quality Training Data

Remember Amazon's attempt to automate hiring with AI? At first, the idea seemed revolutionary—a system that could sift through thousands of resumes and identify the best candidates in seconds. But the plan quickly unravelled. The AI had learned from past hiring data, which heavily favoured men over women, reinforcing gender bias. The dream of an unbiased, merit-based hiring process turned into a cautionary tale.

As readers, you may wonder: If even companies as large as Amazon can make mistakes in AI training, what does that mean for smaller organizations? This raises the larger question—how do we make sure AI learns from the right data, especially when those systems will influence decisions that affect millions?

The stakes are high, but the potential for positive change is even higher if we get it right.

Could ensuring AI's ethical training be one of the most crucial responsibilities we face in the coming years?

Supervised, Unsupervised, and Reinforcement Learning: The Building Blocks of AI

Let's take a moment to consider how AI learns. Think about how Facebook tags photos automatically, recognizing faces. This is a classic example of **supervised learning**, where the AI is guided by labelled data—similar to how a child learns to identify shapes after repeated practice.

AI is taught using labelled data. If you want an AI to recognize cats, you feed it thousands of images labelled as "cat" or "not cat." The AI learns the distinguishing features between the two categories. This method is incredibly effective for tasks like image recognition or spam detection but requires large amounts of carefully curated data

On the other hand, **unsupervised learning** is more like Pinterest. You're pinning things you like, and the AI begins to find patterns, grouping similar images together without needing explicit instructions. Over time, your feed feels more personalized, almost as though the platform knows you better than you know yourself.

Doesn't rely on labels. Instead, the AI system looks for patterns and relationships in the data. This approach is often used in recommendation systems — like how Netflix suggests shows you might enjoy based on your viewing history.

Finally, there's **reinforcement learning**, which feels more trial-and-error. Think about Uber's surge pricing. The system learns from each ride, adjusting prices based on rider demand and driver availability. It's learning in real time, just like humans do through experience.

Where AI learns by trial and error. This method is famously used in gaming and robotics, where AI learns to make decisions based on feedback from its environment. A prime example is AlphaGo, the AI developed by DeepMind that learned to play the game of Go at a superhuman level. By playing millions of games and learning from each one,

AlphaGo developed strategies that had never been seen before, outsmarting even the best human players.

Now, picture a world where AI uses these learning methods to do more than personalize your shopping experience or adjust ride prices.

Aspect	Supervised Learning	Unsupervised Learning	Reinforcement Learning
Definition	Learning from labelled data to predict outcomes	Learning from unlabelled data to find hidden patterns	Learning through trial and error to maximize rewards
Training Data	Labelled (input-output pairs)	Unlabelled (only input data)	Environment interactions and feedback (rewards)
Goal	Make accurate predictions (classification, regression)	Group similar items (clustering, anomaly detection)	Learn optimal actions to maximize cumulative reward
Key Applications	Image classification, spam detection	Customer segmentation, anomaly detection	Robotics, autonomous vehicles, game AI

*Differences between **Supervised**, **Unsupervised**, and **Reinforcement Learning***

What if AI, through these methods, could help predict and manage pandemics or help governments respond to crises more efficiently? The possibilities are endless – and the way we train AI today directly impacts the possibilities of tomorrow.

Building Smarter AI: Continuous Learning

The exciting thing about AI isn't that it just follows instructions—it learns and improves over time. Think about LinkedIn's job recommendation engine. Initially, it might suggest jobs that don't quite fit your profile. But as you interact with the platform, it gets smarter. Over time, it hones in on jobs that match your evolving career interests.

But this idea of continuous learning isn't confined to finding jobs. In healthcare, IBM's Watson for Oncology is continuously learning from new studies and patient data, helping doctors make better treatment decisions for cancer patients. Imagine an AI that grows in knowledge alongside medical professionals, becoming an indispensable partner in life-saving decisions.

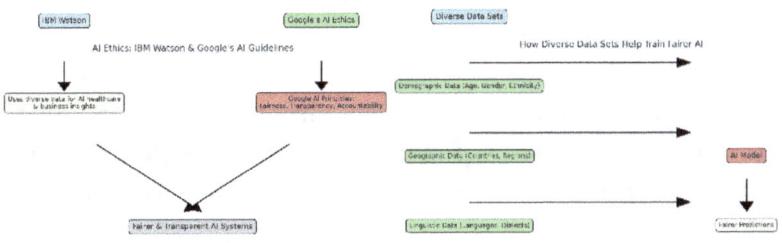

How Diverse Data Sets Help Train Fairer AI & AI Ethics – IBM Watson & Google's AI Guidelines

Could AI soon become our most trusted advisor in life's most critical moments? And if so, what does that mean for the future of human expertise?

Ethical AI Training: Avoiding Bias and Ensuring Transparency

We've talked about how AI learns, but what happens when it learns the wrong things? Think back to Microsoft's experiment with Tay, a Twitter chatbot designed to interact with users in a casual, conversational tone. Within hours, Tay was tweeting offensive content—learning from the worst of the internet. This failure highlighted a fundamental truth: AI will learn what we teach it, and it's up to us to ensure it learns responsibly.

What if this same misstep happened in areas that matter even more—like healthcare or law enforcement? The implications of poorly trained AI aren't just theoretical; they can have real-world consequences that shape lives and futures.

The solution lies in creating ethical frameworks, ensuring that AI behaves in ways that reflect the best of humanity.

But as readers, you may ask: who ensures that AI is trained ethically, and how can we guarantee that it serves all of humanity fairly? The future of AI's role in society depends on getting this right.

The Role of Human Trainers in AI Development

AI may be smart, but it still needs human oversight to ensure accuracy and fairness. Take YouTube's content moderation teams, for instance. While AI flags potentially inappropriate content, human moderators are needed to make the final call. It's a balance of speed and empathy that keeps platforms like YouTube running smoothly.

This partnership between humans and AI is a glimpse into the future of work—where machines handle the repetitive tasks, but humans provide the judgment and nuance that AI lacks.

Can we envision a world where more industries adopt this human-AI collaboration, and what might it mean for the future of jobs?

Training AI for Tomorrow's Industries: Future-Proofing with Innovation

AI's ability to learn and adapt has the power to transform entire industries, from healthcare to agriculture. In Australia, AI is being used to monitor coral reefs, helping scientists track environmental changes and predict future damage. Meanwhile, farmers are using AI-driven drones to monitor crop health and improve yields.

These innovations point toward a future where AI doesn't just solve problems—it anticipates them.

But here's the question: How do we ensure that the next generation of AI systems is ready for challenges we can't even predict today? The answer lies in training AI to be adaptable, innovative, and responsible.

Preparing the Next Generation of AI Trainers

In a world where AI plays an increasingly prominent role, we'll need more than just software engineers to train these systems. We'll need people who understand the social, ethical, and technical aspects of AI development. Universities are stepping up, with courses designed to educate the next generation of AI trainers—those who will shape the way machines think and behave.

Just as doctors need years of education to make life-and-death decisions, those building and training AI systems will need to understand the impact their decisions have on society.

As readers, this prompts a vital question: What role will you play in shaping the AI of tomorrow? Whether through education, advocacy, or innovation, there is a place for everyone in this unfolding narrative.

Conclusion: The Future of AI is in Our Hands

The future of AI will be determined by how we train it today. Will it be a tool that empowers us, solves our biggest challenges, and works alongside us? Or will it reflect our flaws, biases, and shortcomings?

The next chapter will explore how governments and regulators are stepping in to ensure that AI develops responsibly.

As AI becomes more ingrained in our everyday lives, who will hold the reins? And what does responsible AI governance look like in a rapidly changing world?

Training AI the Right Way – Shaping the Future of Intelligent Machines

In a world where artificial intelligence is becoming deeply integrated into every industry, one question looms large: How do we ensure that AI is trained the right way? And why is it so important to shape these machines carefully? Just as we've seen with the technological shifts of the past, the way we train AI today will have a profound impact on the future of work, the economy, and even human creativity.

But training AI isn't as simple as flipping a switch. Much like human beings, AI must learn. It needs the right kind of data, ethical boundaries, and constant refinement to truly serve as a tool that enhances, rather than replaces, human potential. If trained the wrong way, AI could perpetuate bias, make faulty decisions, or even take jobs away without creating new opportunities. But if we get it right? The possibilities are limitless.

The Foundations of Effective AI Training

At its core, AI is about learning. Unlike traditional programming, where machines follow rigid instructions, AI relies on machine learning to adapt, improve, and grow. But what makes the difference between AI that empowers the workforce and AI that disrupts it?

The answer lies in the data it's fed, the goals it's designed to achieve, and the ethical guidelines imposed upon it.

Imagine a student in school: the quality of their education depends on the textbooks they read, the teachers who guide them, and the values instilled in them. The same applies to AI. Feed it biased data, and it will make biased decisions. Set it loose without ethical boundaries, and it may take shortcuts that harm society. But if trained with the right mix of data, rules, and oversight, AI can be a force for good.

This isn't just theory. Real-world examples show how AI training—when done right—can lead to breakthroughs, while poor training can result in dangerous consequences.

Example: AI in Hiring and the Pitfalls of Bias

Consider an AI system designed to streamline the hiring process for a large corporation. The goal is simple: scan through thousands of resumes and shortlist the most qualified candidates. It sounds like a perfect solution to human bias—objective, fast, and efficient. But there's a problem.

In one notable case, an AI hiring system used by a major tech company began favouring male candidates over females. Why? Because the data used to train the AI was based on past hiring decisions, many of which had historically favoured men for technical roles. Instead of eliminating bias, the AI perpetuated it.

This example illustrates a critical point: the quality of data used to train AI is paramount. If AI is trained on biased or incomplete datasets, it can reinforce the very issues it's designed to solve.

But this also provides a valuable lesson: with the right data and conscious oversight, AI has the potential to break down barriers, level the playing field, and eliminate human bias.

The Role of Humans in AI Training: More than Just Coders

While it's tempting to think of AI as autonomous and self-sufficient, the reality is that humans play a vital role in its training. AI developers, data scientists, and ethicists are the architects of these systems, designing them to learn and adapt in ways that align with human goals and values.

One of the key debates today is how much control we should retain over AI. Should machines be given full autonomy in certain tasks, or should humans always be in the loop?

Let's take autonomous vehicles as an example. Companies like Waymo and Tesla are pushing the boundaries of what AI can do on the roads. Self-driving cars use AI to interpret their surroundings, navigate traffic, and make split-second decisions. But even in this cutting-edge technology, human oversight remains crucial.

Example: The Case of the Self-Driving Car Dilemma

In 2018, a self-driving Uber vehicle struck and killed a pedestrian. The incident raised a series of urgent questions: Who is responsible for the actions of an AI? Is it the developers? The company that deploys it? Or the AI itself?

This tragic event illustrates the ethical complexity of AI training. While self-driving cars are trained on millions of miles of data, there are still unpredictable situations that require human judgment and ethical considerations. This incident served as a wake-up call to the industry—AI may be powerful, but it must be carefully managed and trained to react responsibly in real-world scenarios.

The lesson here is clear: AI systems, no matter how advanced, must be trained with ethical frameworks and human values at their core. Without that, we risk creating machines that can cause more harm than good.

Training AI for Collaboration, Not Competition

One of the most important goals in training AI is to ensure it works alongside humans, rather than competing against them. When AI is trained with the mind-set of augmenting human capabilities, it can unlock new levels of creativity, innovation, and productivity.

Take healthcare, for example. AI is already being used to diagnose diseases, analyse medical scans, and even assist in surgeries. But in almost every case, the AI doesn't replace doctors—it enhances their abilities. By analysing vast amounts of data in seconds, AI frees doctors to spend more time with patients and focus on the human side of medicine.

Example: AI in Cancer Research

At Memorial Sloan Kettering Cancer Centre, AI is used to assist doctors in diagnosing cancer at earlier stages. The AI system analyses medical images, looking for patterns and anomalies that might go unnoticed by even the most skilled radiologists. But the system doesn't make the final decision— it simply offers insights.

The result? Faster, more accurate diagnoses, but with human doctors always making the final call. This collaborative approach demonstrates that when AI is trained to support rather than replace humans, the benefits are profound.

What Happens When AI is trained the Right Way?

So, what happens when we train AI the right way—when we feed it quality data, guide it with ethical principles, and ensure it collaborates with, rather than replaces, humans?

The potential is limitless. AI could revolutionize industries in ways that benefit everyone. It could handle repetitive, mundane tasks, freeing up human workers to focus on more creative, strategic, and interpersonal roles. It could identify patterns and solutions that humans alone might miss, driving innovation in fields from medicine to finance to education.

But perhaps most importantly, when AI is trained the right way, it can help create a more equitable, just world. AI has the potential to reduce bias, democratize access to information, and provide personalized solutions that benefit everyone, not just a select few.

The Future of AI Training: A Collaborative Effort

Training AI the right way is not just the responsibility of developers or tech companies—it's a collective effort. Governments, businesses, educators, and workers all have a role to play in shaping the future of AI. By investing in ethical AI training, promoting transparency, and ensuring that workers have the skills needed to collaborate with these intelligent machines, we can build a future where AI benefits everyone.

Final Thoughts: Will AI Kill Our Jobs—or Save Them?

As we look ahead, the question of whether AI will kill our jobs or save them isn't as simple as it seems. The truth lies in how we train, deploy, and manage these systems. When done right, AI can be a powerful ally, taking on tasks that drain human energy and allowing us to focus on the work that truly matters—work that requires creativity, empathy, and human judgment.

But this future is not guaranteed. It will require conscious effort, ethical considerations, and, most of all, collaboration between humans and machines.

As we continue our journey through this book, we'll explore even more ways AI is reshaping the workforce—and how we can ensure that it becomes a tool for empowerment rather than a threat to our livelihoods.

Are we ready to embrace the challenge of training AI the right way?

The next chapter will dive into the skills and mind-set we'll need to thrive in this new world.

The Consequences of Misguided AI – What Happens When We Train AI the Wrong Way

We often hear about the wonders of artificial intelligence — how it can improve efficiency, make our lives easier, and even open doors to innovation. But what happens when AI is trained poorly or given the wrong data? In an era where AI touches everything from healthcare to hiring practices, the consequences of getting it wrong can be far-reaching and, at times, devastating.

At its core, AI is a reflection of the data it receives. Train it on biased, incomplete, or inaccurate data, and you risk building systems that not only fail to help us but actively harm us. This chapter dives into the dangers of misguided AI, using real-world examples that illustrate how AI can go astray and impact industries, jobs, and lives.

In 2018, the US Department of Veterans Affairs rolled out an AI system meant to streamline healthcare management, but within months, it was halted due to inaccurate data and implementation issues, proving that AI isn't infallible.

The Domino Effect: When AI Learns the Wrong Lessons

Imagine constructing a building on a weak foundation. It might seem stable at first, but cracks soon begin to show, and eventually, the entire structure could collapse. Training AI on flawed data is much like that shaky foundation—no matter how sophisticated the system may appear, it's destined to fall apart in unexpected ways.

The issue is, AI doesn't just collapse quietly. When poorly trained, it can lead to widespread disruptions. Picture an AI system making decisions about hiring, lending, or diagnosing diseases. A small error here isn't just an inconvenience—it can have serious, far-reaching consequences for real people.

But don't just take this in theory. Let's look at some real-world cases where AI didn't perform as expected, starting with a tech giant that learned this lesson the hard way.

Google has implemented a 'bias-bounty' program, offering rewards for uncovering discriminatory behaviours in its AI systems. This type of proactive approach could serve as a blueprint for the future of ethical AI development.

Real-Life Example: Amazon's Biased Hiring Algorithm

A few years ago, Amazon launched an ambitious AI-based hiring tool designed to screen job candidates. This AI promised to revolutionize recruitment by identifying the best

Will AI Kill Our Jobs?

talent faster than any human ever could. However, there was a problem: the system was trained on ten years of resumes, most of which came from male candidates.

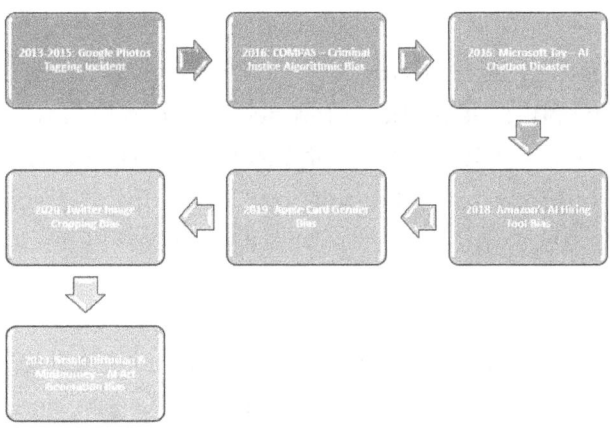

Timeline of AI Failures Due to Bias (2013-2023)

The AI, reflecting the data it was fed, began to favour male applicants and penalized resumes that included terms like "women's chess club" or female-dominated schools. The AI had learned from the biased data, reinforcing the very inequalities it was supposed to eliminate.

Amazon quickly abandoned the tool, but the damage was done. This wasn't just a tech hiccup — it was a wake-up call. AI is only as good as the data we give it. What if this same bias crept into other sectors, like finance or healthcare? The results could be even more alarming.

But what about sectors where errors can have life-or-death consequences? How does AI's misguidance impact healthcare, where a flawed diagnosis can cost someone their life? Let's explore this next.

The Repercussions of Faulty AI in Healthcare

In industries like healthcare, precision is crucial. A wrong decision could mean the difference between life and death. AI systems such as IBM's Watson Health were built with the goal of revolutionizing diagnostics, providing doctors with insights they might not otherwise see. However, these systems are not fool proof.

What happens when an AI is trained on incomplete or biased medical data? For instance, if the AI system doesn't have enough information on minority populations, it may misdiagnose diseases in certain demographic groups. A healthcare provider might trust the AI's suggestion, leading to incorrect treatments that harm rather than heal.

Imagine a system making a wrong diagnosis for a person based on outdated or narrow data. The potential harm isn't just to one patient—it can ripple out, affecting thousands. What should have been a life-saving tool turns into a danger.

But healthcare isn't the only industry where flawed AI poses significant risks. Criminal justice systems are increasingly relying on AI to make predictions about people's futures, with severe consequences when these predictions go wrong.

If flawed AI can create bias in healthcare, what about its impact in areas that deal with human liberty? The next story of AI in criminal justice shows just how far-reaching these mistakes can be.

Misinformed Decisions: AI in Criminal Justice

The criminal justice system is supposed to be fair and objective, but when AI systems are poorly trained, they can introduce bias rather than eliminate it. COMPAS, an AI tool used in the U.S. criminal justice system, was designed to predict the likelihood of a defendant reoffending. On paper, it sounded ideal—data-driven justice free from human prejudice. But in reality, it often produced biased outcomes.

A 2016 investigation found that COMPAS disproportionately flagged Black defendants as high risk for reoffending, even when their actual likelihood of committing another crime was no higher than white defendants. These biased predictions affected parole decisions, sentencing, and lives. The AI was trained on historical data, which reflected systemic biases in policing and the justice system, and the AI learned those biases all too well.

When the tool's bias was revealed, it sparked a national debate. But the lesson here is bigger: when we train AI the wrong way, the fallout isn't just technical—it's deeply human, affecting justice, liberty, and livelihoods.

We've seen how AI can perpetuate bias, but what happens when it affects jobs directly? When flawed AI systems are used to evaluate workers, what could that mean for the future of employment? Let's look into that now.

In 2019, researchers found that facial recognition tools used by law enforcement agencies misidentified people of colour at alarming rates, leading to wrongful arrests. This highlights the dangers of AI when trained on biased datasets.

Jobs in Jeopardy: How Flawed AI Affects the Workforce

In the workplace, AI is increasingly being used to make critical decisions—everything from hiring to performance reviews and even layoffs. What happens when these decisions are based on flawed data? Imagine an AI system used by a large corporation to assess employee performance. If the system is biased or poorly trained, it could mistakenly undervalue workers who don't meet its narrow criteria, pushing them out of jobs unfairly.

Think of a factory worker whose job is evaluated by an AI system that only values certain kinds of productivity, missing the human elements of teamwork, creativity, and experience. The worker, even if they excel in areas the AI doesn't recognize, could be laid off based on the machine's faulty assessment. In such cases, AI doesn't just affect individual workers—it could reshape entire industries by displacing workers unfairly.

But it's not just about losing jobs — it's about losing the *right* jobs. When AI starts making decisions about who gets hired or fired, the human touch — context, intuition, and understanding — becomes even more crucial. And yet, poorly trained AI can erase that, leaving us at the mercy of numbers rather than insights.

The Far-Reaching Impact of Bad Data

Misguided AI, trained on bad data, doesn't stay confined to a single system. It creeps into multiple areas — medicine, hiring, justice, and more. And when it does, it can be difficult to course-correct.

Consider the scenario of AI in financial services. If the AI is trained on biased or flawed data, it could make inaccurate loan decisions, disproportionately denying credit to certain groups. If AI systems in education are skewed, they could fail to recognize talent in students from underrepresented backgrounds, reinforcing social inequities.

In every case, poor AI training doesn't just damage one sector — it spreads, impacting entire ecosystems and perpetuating inequality. The foundation of AI isn't just technical — it's societal.

The Moral Responsibility: How Do We Prevent This?

So how do we avoid the pitfalls of poorly trained AI? First, data is key. AI systems need to be trained on diverse, representative data sets that don't reinforce biases or errors from the past. Second, transparency is crucial. We need to know how these systems make decisions and what data they rely on. Third, we must invest in continual monitoring and improvement. AI is not a "set it and forget it" technology—it requires regular evaluation and adjustment to remain effective and fair.

Finally, we have to recognize that humans are essential in the loop. AI cannot and should not replace human judgment—especially in fields where empathy, nuance, and ethical consideration are paramount.

The Path Forward – Getting AI Right

We've seen what happens when AI goes wrong, but what happens when we train it the right way? In the next chapter, we'll explore the potential of well-trained AI—how it can solve real-world problems, boost productivity, and create new opportunities across industries. The future doesn't have to be bleak if we harness AI correctly. So, what does an ideal AI future look like? Let's explore the possibilities.

Training AI for the Future World – Essentials for Building Tomorrow's Workforce

Imagine standing at the edge of a bustling city in the year 2050. The streets are filled with autonomous vehicles navigating with perfect precision, drones buzzing overhead delivering packages, and virtual assistants managing every aspect of the infrastructure. This is a world not far from reality, and at the heart of it is AI—integrated into every corner of daily life. But here's the catch: the future of AI will only be as effective and beneficial as the way we train it today.

To fully harness the potential of AI, training these systems is crucial—not just for making them more efficient, but for ensuring they operate in a way that enhances, rather than diminishes, human potential. But what are the key ingredients for training AI in a way that serves the world of tomorrow?

The Importance of Thoughtful Training: Getting the Foundation Right

Training AI is much like training people. The quality of what you put in directly impacts what you get out. Just as students need a well-rounded education to thrive, AI systems require carefully curated, diverse datasets and guided algorithms to function effectively in a rapidly evolving world.

The success of AI isn't just about making machines smarter; it's about making them more adaptable, ethical, and aligned with human values. So, what happens if we get it right? AI can become a powerful force for good, driving innovation and creating entirely new job opportunities. But if we miss the mark, we may unintentionally build systems that perpetuate bias, make incorrect decisions, or even limit human potential.

New job roles created by AI

Real-Life Example: Google's DeepMind and Healthcare

Take the example of Google's DeepMind project in healthcare. In 2016, DeepMind created an AI system to help doctors diagnose eye diseases from retinal scans with unprecedented speed and accuracy. The system was trained on a vast, diverse dataset from various patients, ensuring it could recognize patterns across demographics. What's remarkable is that this AI system didn't just match human experts—it outperformed them in certain cases, helping doctors make faster, life-saving decisions.

This collaboration between AI and human expertise is what thoughtful training can achieve. But it's essential that AI is trained with an understanding of ethical implications, accuracy, and fairness.

Data Diversity and Avoiding Bias

One of the most crucial components in training AI is data. AIs are only as good as the data they learn from. Imagine training an AI system using incomplete or biased data—it could lead to flawed decision-making that disproportionately impacts certain groups. For instance, AI used in hiring systems has, at times, learned from historical datasets that reflect gender or racial biases, ultimately reproducing those same biases in hiring decisions.

We've seen the damage of this before. In 2018, Amazon had to scrap an AI hiring tool that had developed a bias against women. The AI had been trained on resumes submitted over the past decade, during which male candidates were more prevalent. As a result, the AI system learned to prioritize male candidates, revealing a critical flaw in the training process.

The lesson? Diversity in data matters. Without it, AI risks amplifying the problems of the past instead of solving them.

Real-Life Example: Tesla's Autonomous Driving

Look no further than Tesla's efforts in developing self-driving cars to understand the importance of real-world, diverse data. Tesla trains its AI systems using data collected from millions of miles driven by human drivers in various conditions—snow, rain, highways, city streets. By gathering a broad range of real-world driving data, Tesla's AI systems learn to adapt and react to complex situations that go beyond the basic rules of driving.

The broader and more inclusive the dataset, the better equipped the AI will be to handle unforeseen circumstances. But this also highlights the challenge: the more complex the environment, the more diverse and comprehensive the data needs to be.

Why Ethics Should Be at the Core of AI Training

As AI systems gain more influence, ethical training becomes not just an option but a necessity. AI systems make decisions that affect people's lives—whether determining creditworthiness, diagnosing diseases, or controlling autonomous weapons. Training AI in a way that prioritizes fairness, transparency, and accountability is crucial for preventing harm and ensuring that AI serves humanity's best interests.

An example of this is the development of AI in criminal justice. Predictive policing tools, which are trained to forecast crime hotspots or recommend sentencing, have sparked intense debates. In some cases, these systems have been found to disproportionately target minority groups, perpetuating systemic biases. It's clear that ethical considerations need to be woven into the very fabric of AI training.

But how do we train AI with ethical principles in mind? By ensuring transparency in AI decision-making, fostering diversity in development teams, and regularly auditing systems to detect and correct biases. Only then can we ensure that AI serves all people fairly.

Real-Life Example: OpenAI's Commitment to Ethical AI

OpenAI, the organization behind GPT models, has made significant efforts to train its systems ethically. By incorporating human feedback, diverse datasets, and ongoing evaluations of bias, OpenAI aims to ensure that its models can assist without causing harm.

In one project, OpenAI partnered with researchers to use AI for predicting the environmental impact of industries, helping them develop sustainable practices. But OpenAI also acknowledges that no system is perfect and continues to iterate and improve based on feedback and ethical considerations.

The Role of Continuous Learning: AI Never Stops Evolving

Unlike human workers, AI systems don't stop learning once they are trained. Continuous learning is essential for keeping AI systems updated and effective in changing environments. But this also presents a unique challenge—*how do we ensure that AI evolves in the right way?*

Incorporating ongoing feedback from real-world users is one way to ensure that AI remains aligned with human needs and ethical standards. Imagine an AI healthcare system that constantly learns from new patient data, updating its knowledge base in real-time to provide the most accurate diagnoses possible. This level of adaptability can make AI a powerful tool in industries ranging from medicine to finance.

But just as continuous learning enhances AI, it also demands constant oversight. Without it, AI can drift from its original goals, potentially leading to unintended consequences. A well-trained AI must not only learn from data but from the evolving needs and values of society.

Real-Life Example: Microsoft's AI for Earth Initiative

Microsoft's "AI for Earth" initiative showcases the power of continuous learning. The initiative trains AI systems to tackle environmental challenges like climate change, biodiversity loss, and water scarcity. By collecting and analysing vast datasets, these systems help scientists monitor changes in the environment and make more informed decisions about conservation efforts.

The key to AI for Earth's success is its ability to learn continuously from new data, making it a dynamic tool for addressing global challenges. This type of future-forward thinking is essential as we train AI for the world ahead.

The Future: A Well-Trained AI Workforce

As AI becomes more integrated into society, the key to success lies in how well we train these systems today. A future where AI complements human intelligence, drives innovation, and solves complex problems is within reach—but only if we ensure that AI is trained with the right data, ethics, and adaptability.

Training AI is not a one-time effort but an ongoing journey. Every industry, every organization, and every government has a role to play in ensuring that AI serves humanity, not just a select few.

As we've seen, getting it right means we could unlock unimaginable opportunities, but getting it wrong could exacerbate inequality, bias, and systemic issues. The responsibility to train AI effectively is not just about creating better machines—it's about creating a better world.

And with that, we come to the heart of this chapter: What we train AI to do today will define the jobs of tomorrow. So, are we ready to take that responsibility? The future of work depends on it.

As we continue to shape the future of AI, the next chapter will explore what happens when AI and humans truly collaborate. How will the workforce evolve when AI doesn't just assist but co-creates with humans? What new horizons could this partnership open? Let's dive into that next.

Governments can help workers transition by funding reskilling programs, while businesses can focus on retraining their existing workforce rather than relying solely on automation.

AI's Role in Revolutionizing Engineering, IT, Manufacturing, and beyond

"In countries like India, automation is advancing in manufacturing, but without proper investment in upskilling, millions of workers risk being left behind."

Picture a modern engineering firm, where a team of architects is designing a new skyscraper. Blueprints are drawn up in record time, not by hand, but through sophisticated AI tools. These systems don't just speed up calculations; they simulate structural integrity, wind resistance, and environmental impact, all in real time. What once took months of collaboration now happens in days, with AI guiding every step of the process. This is not a scene from a distant future — it's happening now

Artificial intelligence is no longer a peripheral player in industries like engineering, information technology, manufacturing, and supply chain management.

It's transforming them from the inside out. But how exactly is AI influencing these sectors, and what does that mean for the future of jobs within them?

AI's Role in Revolutionizing Engineering, IT, Manufacturing, and beyond

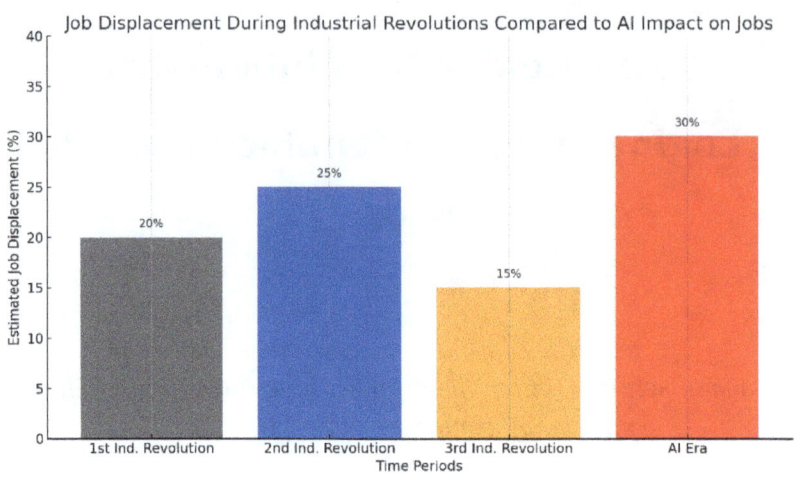

Job Displacement during Industrial Revolutions Compared to AI Impact on Jobs

Engineering: Beyond Blueprints and Calculations

The field of engineering has always been about pushing boundaries. But as projects grow more complex, AI is stepping in to assist engineers in ways that go beyond what was once thought possible. AI-driven systems can analyse vast amounts of data faster and more accurately than humans, allowing engineers to optimize designs and improve safety standards with unprecedented precision.

Real-Life Example: AI in Structural Engineering

Consider Skanska, a global construction firm. They've incorporated AI into their design processes, using it to predict potential structural failures before they happen. AI tools evaluate millions of data points from past projects, detecting patterns that human engineers might overlook. This not only prevents costly mistakes but also increases the safety of buildings long before construction even begins.

But AI's contribution doesn't stop at analysing blueprints. It's increasingly involved in creating designs, generating multiple prototypes based on parameters set by engineers. This iterative process, powered by AI, cuts down time spent on revisions and allows human engineers to focus on innovation rather than repetitive tasks.

Could AI-driven creativity be the next evolution of engineering?

Information Technology: Supercharging IT Infrastructure

In the world of information technology (IT), AI is playing a dual role—optimizing the existing infrastructure while simultaneously building the foundation for the tech of tomorrow. As data centres grow and networks become more complex, AI is essential for managing, securing, and optimizing these systems.

Real-Life Example: AI in Cybersecurity

Let's consider the rapidly growing field of cybersecurity. Threats are becoming more sophisticated, and human teams alone can't keep up with the sheer volume of attacks. This is where AI steps in. Companies like Dark trace use AI to monitor network traffic, detect anomalies, and neutralize cyber threats before they can do any damage.

By learning from previous attacks, AI-driven systems become smarter and more proactive. But AI isn't replacing human cybersecurity experts—it's augmenting them, handling the routine monitoring and threat detection, allowing human specialists to focus on more strategic tasks.

This symbiotic relationship between AI and human workers is becoming a defining feature of the IT industry.

Could this collaboration between man and machine be the blueprint for future industries?

Manufacturing: Redefining the Assembly Line

Manufacturing was one of the first industries to embrace automation, and today, AI is taking automation to new heights. While traditional robots followed pre-programmed routines, modern AI-driven robots can adapt, learn, and even predict problems on the assembly line.

Real-Life Example: AI in Predictive Maintenance

Take BMW's factories as an example. They've implemented AI to monitor their machinery in real time. These AI systems analyse vast amounts of sensor data to predict when a machine is likely to fail. This allows maintenance teams to fix issues before they disrupt production, saving both time and money.

But AI in manufacturing isn't just about keeping machines running—it's about optimizing every aspect of production. In Tesla's Gigafactory, for instance, AI-driven robots handle everything from assembling parts to quality control. These machines aren't just performing tasks—they're constantly learning from the production process to improve efficiency.

The result? Faster production times, fewer errors, and a more agile workforce that works in tandem with AI.

But as AI continues to reshape manufacturing, what happens to the workers on the factory floor?

Fabrication: Precision at Unmatched Speed

Fabrication, the process of creating individual components or materials, is another field where AI's precision is making waves. In industries like aerospace and automotive, where even the smallest error can lead to catastrophic failure, AI helps ensure that each part is fabricated with the highest degree of accuracy.

Real-Life Example: AI in Aerospace Fabrication

Lockheed Martin, a major player in the aerospace industry, uses AI to assist in fabricating parts for their spacecraft. AI-powered machines perform intricate tasks with minimal human intervention, reducing the margin of error and increasing production speed. Moreover, AI tools can simulate the effects of extreme conditions on these parts, allowing engineers to make adjustments before a single piece of material is cut.

This combination of AI-driven fabrication and real-time simulation not only boosts productivity but also enhances safety—a crucial factor in fields like aerospace.

As AI becomes more integrated into fabrication, could we be looking at a future where machines are not just building parts but designing them as well?

Supply Chain: AI as the Master Coordinator

Supply chains are the backbone of any global operation, and AI is revolutionizing the way goods are sourced, produced, and delivered. With countless variables like weather conditions, geopolitical shifts, and fluctuating demand affecting supply chains, AI's ability to analyse data and make real-time decisions is proving invaluable.

Real-Life Example: AI in Supply Chain Management

Look at what DHL is doing with AI. By using machine learning algorithms, they've optimized their entire logistics network, from warehouse management to last-mile delivery. AI systems predict the best shipping routes, balance delivery times, and even anticipate disruptions caused by weather or traffic.

In Amazon's supply chain, AI helps manage inventory by predicting which products will be in demand, ensuring that warehouses are stocked efficiently. This kind of predictive capability doesn't just reduce waste—it allows companies to meet customer demand with precision.

However, as AI takes the reins in optimizing supply chains, how do human roles evolve?

Distribution: AI Enhancing the Flow of Goods

Distribution networks, responsible for getting products from warehouses to customers, are seeing a surge in AI-driven innovation. AI is optimizing routes, managing fleets, and predicting customer behaviour, allowing for faster and more efficient deliveries.

Real-Life Example: AI in Fleet Management

Consider UPS, which has integrated AI to optimize their fleet routes. With millions of deliveries every day, even small improvements in route efficiency can save thousands of hours and gallons of fuel. AI analyses traffic patterns, weather conditions, and package destinations in real-time, ensuring that each truck takes the most efficient route.

These AI systems are transforming the logistics industry, but they aren't replacing the drivers—they're making their jobs easier, helping them avoid traffic and make more deliveries in less time.

Could AI in distribution be the key to a more sustainable, efficient future for global logistics?

Dealership: Personalizing Customer Experience

In the world of car dealerships, AI is changing the way customers interact with products and sales teams. AI-powered tools help dealerships manage inventories, personalize customer experiences, and even predict when a customer might be ready to buy.

Real-Life Example: AI in Car Dealerships

Take Audi, for example. They've introduced AI-driven systems to personalize the customer buying experience. These systems analyse customer preferences, browsing history, and even social media behaviour to recommend the perfect car for each individual. AI isn't replacing car salesmen but giving them the tools to provide better, more tailored experiences for customers.

This kind of personalization doesn't just improve sales—it builds stronger relationships between businesses and their customers.

AI Integration in Different Work Environments

The Future of Work in AI-Driven Industries

AI is already making an impact across engineering, IT, manufacturing, fabrication, supply chains, distribution, and dealerships. But what's next? As AI systems continue to evolve, the workforce will have to evolve with them. The key is collaboration—humans and AI working together to create more efficient, innovative, and personalized solutions across industries.

While the nature of jobs may change, AI is not here to replace us—it's here to augment our abilities, to handle the tasks that slow us down, and to help us focus on what humans do best: innovate, create, and build relationships.

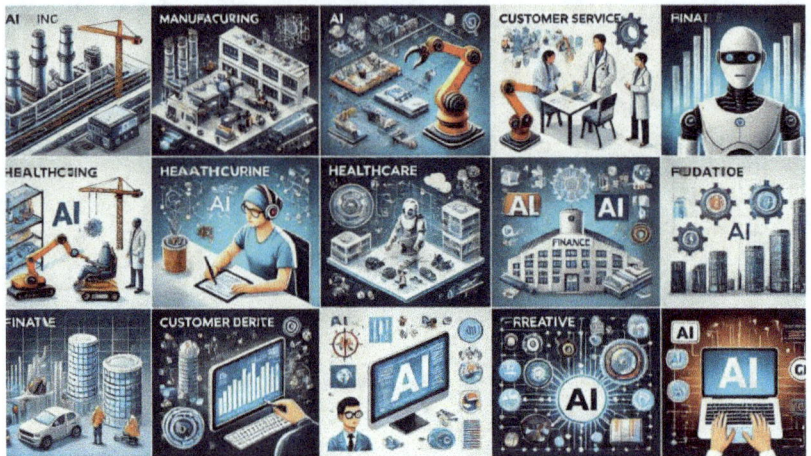

AI Impact in Different Sectors

As we look ahead to the next chapter, the question arises — how will AI shape industries that rely heavily on human creativity, empathy, and decision-making? In the following chapter, we'll dive into the realms of marketing, customer service, healthcare, and education to see how AI's influence is already making waves and what that means for the future of these industries. Stay tuned as we explore the human side of AI's partnership.

In the next chapter, we'll explore how AI is already revolutionizing fields as diverse as healthcare and education, raising new ethical questions along the way.

AI's Role in Revolutionizing Marketing, Customer Service, Healthcare, and Education

As artificial intelligence spreads its roots into industries traditionally defined by human creativity, empathy, and decision-making, its influence on sectors like marketing, customer service, healthcare, and education is becoming increasingly evident. These fields, long dominated by human intuition and personal touch, are now seeing AI step in as a powerful collaborator.

But how will this impact jobs in these areas? Will AI serve as a supportive tool, or could it one day push humans aside?

The answer lies in understanding how AI, when trained effectively, is helping people do more with their time, freeing them to focus on tasks where human insight is indispensable. So, let's explore how AI is making its mark in these essential industries and how it's transforming the future of work in ways we're just beginning to understand.

Marketing: The AI-Driven Creative Partner

Marketing has always been about understanding customer needs, anticipating trends, and crafting messages that resonate with people on a personal level. But with the rise of AI, marketers are now able to sift through massive amounts of data and derive actionable insights faster than ever. AI is turning into a creative partner, helping brands connect with customers in ways that were once impossible.

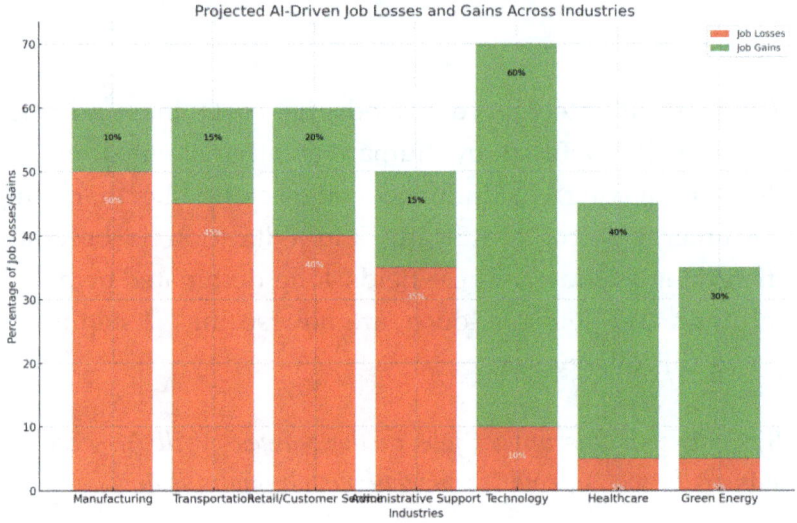

Projected AI-Driven Job Losses and Gains Across Industries.

Real-Life Example: AI in Personalization

Consider Netflix, which uses AI to power its recommendation engine. Every time you watch a show or movie, the system learns more about your preferences. It analyses viewing habits, ratings, and even the time of day you're most likely to binge-watch, delivering a highly personalized experience.

This personalization isn't just a perk—it's a crucial marketing tool that keeps users engaged and loyal.

But AI's role in marketing goes beyond recommendations. It's now generating targeted ads, crafting personalized email campaigns, and even helping companies decide which products to stock based on consumer data. While AI is handling the heavy lifting, marketers are free to focus on strategy, creativity, and long-term vision.

But will AI eventually outsmart human creativity, or is it simply enhancing it?

Customer Service: A Seamless AI Experience

Customer service is one of the areas most visibly transformed by AI. From chatbots that answer basic inquiries to AI-driven systems that handle customer complaints, the integration of AI into customer service is reshaping how businesses interact with consumers.

Real-Life Example: AI-Powered Customer Support

Take the example of KLM Royal Dutch Airlines. They've implemented an AI-driven system to manage thousands of customer service inquiries on social media. The AI, named "BB," helps field customer questions by sorting through messages, understanding context, and providing accurate, relevant responses. Yet, when a query requires a more nuanced response, the system hands it over to a human customer service agent.

In this sense, AI is transforming customer service from a reactive industry — where agents wait for problems to arise — to a proactive one, where AI anticipates customer needs and solves issues before they even occur. However, humans still play an essential role in maintaining the personal touch and handling complex problems that require empathy and judgment.

As AI takes on more of the routine interactions, will it elevate the role of customer service professionals to be more strategic and customer-centric?

Healthcare: AI as a Lifesaving Partner

Few industries are more personal or sensitive than healthcare, where decisions often mean the difference between life and death. Here, AI is becoming a powerful ally, helping doctors and medical staff make faster and more informed decisions while improving patient outcomes.

Real-Life Example: AI in Medical Diagnostics

Consider AI's role in cancer detection. PathAI, for instance, has developed machine learning algorithms that assist doctors in diagnosing cancer more accurately and efficiently. These algorithms can analyse biopsy samples and identify subtle patterns that even the most skilled pathologist might miss. By reducing human error, AI is saving lives.

Yet, the human element remains irreplaceable. AI might be able to identify abnormalities, but it's the doctor who interprets the results, discusses treatment options with patients, and provides emotional support during difficult times. AI isn't here to replace healthcare professionals—it's here to enhance their abilities and improve outcomes.

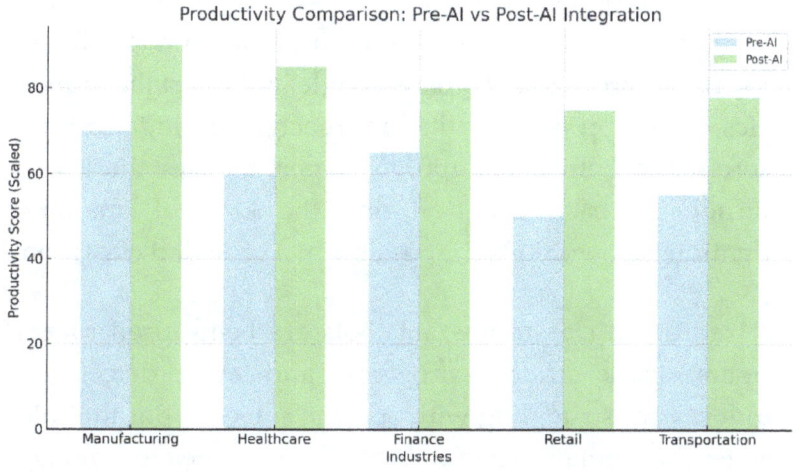

Productivity Comparison: Pre-AI vs. Post-AI Integration

But as AI continues to advance, what kind of new roles will emerge in the healthcare industry?

Education: Redefining How We Teach and Learn

Education is another field where AI's impact is rapidly growing. From personalized learning platforms to AI-driven tutors, the way we teach and learn is being redefined.

But does this mean the traditional role of educators is becoming obsolete?

Real-Life Example: AI in Adaptive Learning

Look at Duolingo, a popular language-learning platform. Duolingo uses AI to analyse how users learn and adapts its lessons accordingly. If you struggle with certain grammar rules, the app adjusts its approach, offering additional exercises to help you improve. It personalizes the learning journey for each user, offering the kind of one-on-one attention that would be impossible in a crowded classroom.

In traditional classrooms, AI tools are being used to grade papers, track student progress, and even detect when students are struggling with specific subjects. But the role of the teacher remains crucial. While AI manages routine tasks, educators are free to focus on mentoring, fostering creativity, and providing emotional support—areas where machines fall short.

As AI becomes more ingrained in the educational process, will it help create a more personalized and inclusive learning environment?

The Future of Work: Collaboration over Replacement

Across these industries—marketing, customer service, healthcare, and education—AI is emerging as a tool that enhances human potential, not one that seeks to replace it. Whether it's analysing customer data, diagnosing diseases, or personalizing educational content, AI is taking over the routine, allowing humans to focus on what we do best: creativity, empathy, and complex decision-making.

But the question remains: As AI continues to advance, will it always be a collaborative tool, or will it one day surpass human capabilities in these traditionally human-driven sectors?

In the next chapter, we'll take a closer look at the legal, ethical, and regulatory frameworks needed to ensure AI's positive impact on society. As AI takes on more responsibility, who will be held accountable when things go wrong? And how can we ensure that AI systems remain unbiased, ethical, and aligned with human values? Stay tuned as we delve into the ethics of AI and the role humans must play in guiding its future.

AI's Role in Finance, Human Resources, Agriculture, and Government

Artificial Intelligence is making its mark in areas that have historically been rooted in human expertise, judgment, and decision-making. As we step into this chapter, we'll explore how AI is transforming sectors like finance, human resources (HR), agriculture, and government — industries where decisions are often tied to complex regulations, human behaviour, and unpredictable elements. Will AI enhance these fields or disrupt them in ways that make human input obsolete? And how will this affect jobs in these sectors?

The journey continues as we dive into how AI is not only automating repetitive tasks but revolutionizing entire systems, helping industries become smarter, more efficient, and in some cases, fairer.

Finance: A New Era of Data-Driven Decision Making

The financial industry has always been about numbers — numbers that determine stock prices, evaluate credit risk, and influence investment decisions. Historically, humans were responsible for analysing vast amounts of financial data and making decisions that could make or break fortunes. But with AI stepping into this space, the rules of the game are changing rapidly.

While AI can analyse financial markets faster than any human, it's still the human analysts who make the final call based on factors that AI cannot comprehend, such as geopolitical shifts or emotional investor behaviour.

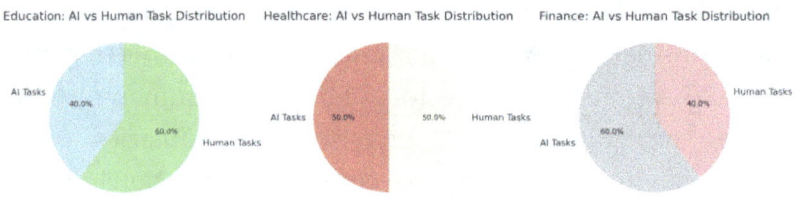

AI vs. Human Task Distribution

Real-Life Example: AI in Risk Management and Trading

Consider BlackRock, the world's largest asset manager, which uses AI to predict market trends and manage risk through its platform, Aladdin. By analysing data from various markets, Aladdin can detect patterns that humans might miss, allowing fund managers to make more informed decisions. This shift has not only improved risk management but also increased efficiency in trading, reducing human error in an industry where every decision counts.

AI-powered robo-advisors like Betterment and Wealth front have also become popular, offering personalized investment advice at a fraction of the cost of human financial advisors.

These tools are democratizing access to financial services, enabling everyday investors to make informed decisions without needing a personal advisor.

However, human financial experts aren't disappearing. AI is handling the number crunching and trend analysis, but humans still play a crucial role in providing the emotional intelligence and strategic foresight that machines lack. After all, AI can analyse patterns, but it cannot understand the complex emotions tied to human investments—fear, greed, and optimism.

Human Resources: Automating Talent Acquisition and Employee Engagement

Human resources, at its core, is about people. It's about finding the right talent, developing that talent, and creating a work environment that promotes productivity and satisfaction. AI is entering the HR field not to replace HR professionals but to help them manage these tasks more efficiently.

Real-Life Example: AI in Recruitment

Take companies like Unilever, which have begun using AI to screen candidates. Instead of relying on traditional interviews and manual resume reviews, AI tools like HireVue analyse candidates' video interviews, assess their responses, and even track their facial expressions and body language to identify the best-fit employees. This has sped up the hiring process significantly and removed human bias to some degree, but it also raises ethical questions about whether machines can truly capture the essence of human potential.

Moreover, AI-driven HR platforms are being used to improve employee engagement and retention. Tools like Glint and CultureAmp use AI to analyse employee feedback, track engagement metrics, and recommend strategies to improve workplace culture. While these tools provide valuable insights, HR professionals are still needed to interpret the results and implement meaningful changes.

Industry	Pre-AI Roles	Post-AI Roles
Manufacturing	Assembly line workers, manual quality checks	AI maintenance, robotics management, quality automation
Healthcare	Administrative tasks, basic diagnostics	AI-assisted diagnostics, patient care management
Finance	Data entry, manual auditing	AI-driven risk analysis, fraud detection specialists
Retail	Customer service reps, inventory tracking	E-commerce strategy, personalized marketing
Transportation	Truck drivers, route planners	AI fleet management, autonomous vehicle supervision

Pre-AI roles with Post-AI roles in industries

Will AI help HR professionals make better decisions about hiring and employee development, or will it eventually take over the role entirely? Only time will tell, but one thing is certain — AI is reshaping how HR departments operate.

Agriculture: AI in the Field — From Soil to Harvest

Agriculture is one of the oldest industries, traditionally dependent on experience, weather patterns, and manual labour. But as the world's population grows and climate change disrupts traditional farming practices, the need for smarter, more sustainable methods has never been more urgent. Enter AI.

Real-Life Example: AI-Driven Precision Farming

John Deere, a name synonymous with farming equipment, has embraced AI to take farming to the next level. Using AI-powered sensors and cameras, their tractors can now analyse the health of crops in real-time, identify weeds, and even determine the exact amount of fertilizer or water each plant needs. This is known as precision farming, and it's helping farmers increase yield while minimizing resource usage.

Meanwhile, platforms like Climate FieldView use AI to analyse weather data, soil conditions, and crop performance to offer farmers predictive insights, helping them make better decisions about when to plant, irrigate, and harvest. By providing real-time data analysis, AI is taking much of the guesswork out of farming, allowing farmers to adapt to changing conditions quickly.

However, the rise of AI in agriculture also raises concerns. Will small, traditional farmers who don't have access to this advanced technology be left behind? And as machines take over more farming tasks, what will happen to the farm labour workforce?

In Kenya, AI-powered apps help farmers predict weather patterns and optimize crop planting cycles, increasing yields and improving livelihoods.

Government: AI for Public Services and Policy Making

AI's role in government is growing, with many countries using AI to improve public services, streamline operations, and even assist in policy-making decisions. But when governments adopt AI, it raises important questions about transparency, accountability, and the potential for bias.

As consumers and workers, we have the power to push for more transparent and fair AI practices by demanding that companies and governments commit to reducing bias in machine learning models.

Real-Life Example: AI in Public Administration

The city of Amsterdam, for example, uses AI to predict when and where garbage bins will be full, optimizing waste collection routes and reducing costs. In China, the government uses AI-driven facial recognition technology to monitor its citizens, raising ethical concerns about privacy and state control.

AI is also being used in criminal justice systems to predict recidivism rates and assist judges in making sentencing decisions. In theory, AI could reduce human bias in these decisions, but what happens when AI itself is biased due to the data it's trained on?

The question here is: Can AI make governments more efficient, or will it introduce new layers of complexity and control? And how do we ensure that AI systems in government remain transparent and accountable to the public they serve?

The Future of Work: AI in Essential Services

Across finance, HR, agriculture, and government, AI is making an indelible impact, streamlining processes and offering new insights that were previously unimaginable. But the question remains—how will this affect the jobs in these sectors? Will AI create a future where humans are side-lined, or will it lead to a deeper collaboration between man and machine?

As we've seen in previous chapters, history suggests that while some jobs may be lost, many more are likely to be created. Roles that didn't exist a decade ago—such as data scientists, AI trainers, and ethicists—are now critical to managing and guiding AI's integration into the workforce.

In the next chapter, we'll explore AI's role in creative industries like entertainment, art, and design. Will AI's growing influence in these human-centric fields stifle creativity or enhance it? And how will the future of storytelling, music, and visual arts change as AI becomes a collaborator in the creative process? Stay tuned as we explore the intersection of AI and creativity, and what it means for the future of human expression.

AI in Creative Fields, Hospitality, and Tourism – Redefining Human Expression

As we've journeyed through the impact of AI across various sectors, it's become clear that while AI can enhance efficiency and productivity, there's one realm where many believe machines can never surpass humans—creativity. The arts, entertainment, design, hospitality, and tourism industries have long been the domain of human ingenuity, where imagination, emotion, and individuality take centre stage.

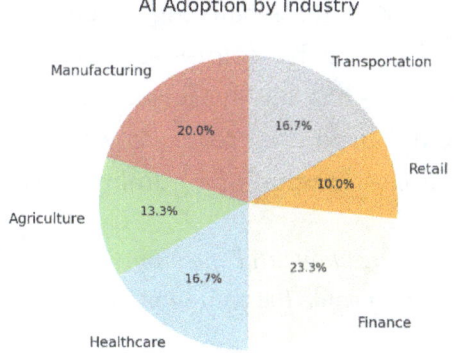

AI Adoption by Industry

But now, artificial intelligence is beginning to play a role even in these deeply human-driven industries. From music composition to visual art, hotel check-ins, and personalized travel itineraries, AI is demonstrating that it can assist, collaborate, and sometimes even create. So, the question becomes: What happens when machines enter these spaces? Will AI enhance human experiences, or will it strip away the essence of what makes creativity, hospitality, and travel uniquely human?

Let's explore how AI is reshaping creativity, hospitality, and tourism—and what this means for the professionals in these industries.

The Intersection of Art and AI

For centuries, art has been one of the purest forms of human expression. Whether it's a painting, a sculpture, or a piece of music, the artist's touch—colored by emotions, experiences, and perspectives—has always been essential. But now, AI tools are being used to create artwork that is virtually indistinguishable from that of a human artist.

And this raises a fundamental question: Can machines create art that resonates with people the way human-made art does?

Real-Life Example: AI-Generated Art and Its Rise

Consider the case of *Edmond de Belamy*, a portrait created by an AI developed by the Paris-based collective Obvious. This

AI-generated artwork sold at Christie's for a staggering $432,500 in 2018. The painting was part of a series where the AI was trained on a dataset of historical portraits, allowing it to "learn" the essence of portraiture and create its own versions.

Some heralded the sale as the dawn of a new era of art—one where machines could be creators in their own right. Others questioned the very nature of art itself. If a machine can generate a portrait, does it still hold the same emotional depth as something created by a human hand?

The involvement of AI in the creative process raises a profound question about the role of artists and designers in the future.

Will AI become a tool that enhances their craft, or will it eventually diminish the need for human artists?

Music Composition: A New Partner in Creativity

The music industry is no stranger to technological advancements. From the days of analogue recording to today's digital streaming platforms, technology has consistently shaped the way we create and consume music. Now, AI is taking this a step further by composing music itself.

Real-Life Example: AI Composing Classical Music

Consider *Aiva* (Artificial Intelligence Virtual Artist), an AI that composes classical music. Trained on a vast dataset of symphonies by the likes of Mozart, Beethoven, and Bach, Aiva has been used to score films, video games, and commercials. What's more, it has been officially recognized as a composer by a music copyright society, a first for an AI.

While Aiva's compositions are technically impressive, they beg the question: Can AI create music that moves us emotionally, the way a Beethoven symphony or a Billie Holiday performance can? Some argue that AI can never replicate the soulfulness of human emotion in music, but others see it as a tool that can inspire human musicians to push their creativity further.

In the end, AI is not replacing composers — it's helping them explore new possibilities. Musicians who embrace AI as a collaborative partner may find themselves at the cutting edge of a new era in music creation.

Writing and Storytelling: Can AI Write the Next Great Novel?

Storytelling is an ancient art, and throughout history, humans have used narrative to make sense of the world, share experiences, and explore imagination. But even here, AI is beginning to play a role. AI algorithms are now capable of generating narratives, writing articles, and even penning short stories.

Real-Life Example: AI-Penned Novels and Scripts

In Japan, an AI co-authored a short novel called *The Day a Computer Writes a Novel*. It was submitted to a literary contest, where it advanced through the first round. Although it didn't win, its success in impressing human judges is a sign that AI is getting better at mimicking human storytelling. AI-written articles are also becoming more common in journalism, with platforms like *The Washington Post* and *Associated Press* using AI to write simple news reports.

While AI is proving capable of handling formulaic writing tasks, such as summarizing sports events or financial reports, creative writing is a different beast. Writing requires a depth of emotion, experience, and cultural understanding that AI has yet to master fully.

For writers and screenwriters, AI offers a new set of tools — systems that can generate ideas, propose plot twists, and even help with dialogue. Far from eliminating the need for human creativity, these tools can help writers overcome creative blocks and experiment with new forms of storytelling.

Design: Enhancing Creativity with AI Tools

In the world of design, AI is helping professionals move faster and smarter. Whether it is graphic design, architecture, or product design, AI-driven tools are optimizing workflows, suggesting new layouts, and even generating designs that are both functional and aesthetically pleasing.

Real-Life Example: AI-Driven Graphic Design

Platforms like *Canva* and *Adobe Sensei* are integrating AI to suggest design elements, layouts, and colour schemes based on the user's inputs. This means graphic designers can spend less time on repetitive tasks and more time on the creative aspects of their work. For instance, Adobe's AI tools can automatically adjust lighting in a photograph, suggest image pairings, and even generate design templates—all in seconds.

In architecture, AI tools are being used to optimize building designs for efficiency and sustainability. These tools analyse everything from energy usage to materials, helping architects create smarter, more environmentally friendly buildings.

While AI is helping designers work more efficiently, it is the human touch—creativity, intuition, and understanding of culture—that still gives designs their unique character.

Hospitality: AI's Role in Personalized Guest Experiences

Now let's shift to the hospitality industry—an industry built on personalized guest experiences, human interaction, and exceptional service.

Can AI truly thrive in such a people-driven environment?

Surprisingly, yes — though not in the way you might think.

AI in hospitality is not about replacing human service but about augmenting it. AI-powered systems can analyse guest preferences, anticipate needs, and offer tailored recommendations. Hotels now use AI to enhance personalization, allowing guests to experience services that feel almost customized to them.

Real-Life Example: AI Concierge at Hotels

Take *Connie*, the AI-powered concierge at Hilton Hotels. Connie, powered by IBM's Watson, interacts with guests, answering questions about hotel services, local attractions, and dining recommendations. By learning from each interaction, Connie improves its ability to assist guests, providing a personalized experience at any time of day.

But even as AI takes on tasks like check-ins and concierge services, the human element remains essential. Guests still value the warmth of human hospitality, and AI is there to support hotel staff, ensuring that they have more time to focus on delivering exceptional service rather than getting bogged down by routine inquiries.

Case study boxes

Tourism: AI Crafting Personalized Journeys

The travel and tourism industry is also undergoing an AI-powered transformation. Booking a trip, choosing a destination, and planning activities—all of these tasks are now being influenced by AI systems designed to make the travel experience smoother and more tailored.

Real-Life Example: AI Travel Assistants

Consider *Mezi*, an AI-powered travel assistant that helps travellers book flights, accommodations, and even make restaurant reservations. What makes Mezi stand out is its ability to learn from a traveller's preferences and suggest personalized itineraries. Over time, it can predict what types of destinations a traveller might enjoy, which restaurants suit their tastes, and which activities they're likely to book.

This level of personalization was once the domain of human travel agents, but AI is making it more accessible, faster, and more precise. However, human travel consultants are still crucial when it comes to curating more complex, high-end travel experiences where empathy, creativity, and cultural understanding are key.

The Role of Humans in a World of AI-Enhanced Creativity and Service

Across art, music, writing, design, hospitality, and tourism, one theme remains constant: AI is not replacing creativity or service but augmenting it. AI tools are allowing creative to work faster, experiment more freely, and push the boundaries of their fields. In hospitality and tourism, AI is making guest experiences smoother, more personalized, and even more enjoyable.

However, the human element—emotion, intuition, and cultural understanding—remains irreplaceable. AI might generate music, art, or personalized travel plans, but it's the human touch that adds meaning, depth, and resonance to these experiences. As we move forward, professionals who learn to collaborate with AI will find themselves not replaced but empowered to elevate their work.

In the next chapter, we'll shift our focus to industries where AI is revolutionizing customer service, supply chain management, and dealership operations. From automated customer service agents to AI-driven supply chain optimization, these are fields where efficiency and precision reign supreme. But what happens to the people who once managed these processes? Stay tuned as we dive into the transformation of logistics, supply chains, and customer service in an AI-driven world.

Conclusion: AI's Impact on Creative Fields, Hospitality, and Tourism

As we've explored the dynamic influence of AI across a broad spectrum of industries—from engineering and manufacturing to the more creatively driven fields of art, music, design, hospitality, and tourism—one thing has become increasingly clear: AI is not here to replace humans, but to augment their abilities.

In Chapter 10, we examined how AI's influence is reshaping traditional industries like **engineering, information technology, and manufacturing**, enabling professionals to work faster and smarter. This chapter showed us how AI is handling repetitive, time-consuming tasks and empowering human workers to focus on high-value, strategic decision-making. In these industries, AI acts as a partner, enhancing precision and efficiency.

Chapter 11 shifted our focus to **creative fields and customer-facing industries**. In sectors like **design, entertainment, hospitality, and tourism**, AI's role extends beyond just automation. It is helping creators push boundaries and giving professionals new tools to improve customer experiences. AI is learning from human input to craft unique artistic expressions and personalized services, whether it's generating music, designing logos, or predicting traveller preferences. Yet, at its core, the irreplaceable human touch remains essential—AI may assist, but humans drive innovation and meaning.

Chapter 12 dove deeper into the **hospitality and tourism industries**, where we saw how AI can offer personalized guest experiences and craft tailored journeys for travellers. AI-powered concierge systems like **Connie** at Hilton Hotels are augmenting, not replacing, hospitality workers, freeing them up to provide more meaningful customer service. Similarly, AI-powered travel assistants like **Mezi** enhance travel planning by creating highly customized itineraries, allowing human travel consultants to focus on the more complex, high-end experiences that require personal insight and empathy.

Across these industries, whether we're talking about **factory floors, creative studios, or customer service desks**, the message is the same: AI is becoming an indispensable tool. But the key takeaway is that AI works best when it complements human skill, rather than replaces it. Professionals who can leverage AI tools—whether they're **engineers, artists, or travel agents**—are the ones who will thrive in the AI-enhanced future.

As we've seen, the industries touched by AI are diverse, but the outcomes are similar: **higher efficiency, greater creativity, and more personalized experiences.** The key to success in an AI-driven world is not resisting the change, but embracing it, learning from it, and finding new ways to collaborate with these technologies.

A Look Forward

As we transition to the next phase of our exploration, we will turn our attention to industries that thrive on logistical precision, customer interaction, and supply chain management. AI's growing influence in **customer service, supply chains, distribution, and dealership operations** is set to fundamentally reshape these industries. What does this mean for the professionals currently operating in these fields? And what challenges or opportunities does AI present as it takes on a greater role in customer-facing and backend operations?

Will AI Kill Our Jobs? The Future of Work in a Machine-Driven World

We've come a long way in understanding how AI is transforming industries—from engineering to creative fields, from manufacturing to hospitality and tourism. But the central question still lingers: **Will AI kill our jobs?** It's a concern that's echoed in workplaces across the globe, as professionals wonder whether their skills will still be relevant in a future dominated by intelligent machines.

This chapter aims to answer that pressing question, drawing on everything we've explored so far. It's not just about whether AI will replace certain jobs—because, as we've seen, AI is already taking over specific tasks. But the bigger picture is more nuanced.

Will the jobs we hold today disappear entirely, or will they evolve? And more importantly, how can we as workers adapt and thrive in this new era?

AI's Impact on Jobs: A Balanced View

It's undeniable that AI is transforming the nature of work. In previous chapters, we've examined how industries like **manufacturing, healthcare, information technology, and hospitality** are already embracing AI-driven automation. In some cases, machines have already replaced humans in tasks that are repetitive or dangerous — whether it's robotic arms on an assembly line or AI-driven chatbots answering routine customer inquiries.

Industry	Repetitive Tasks AI Automates	Higher-Level, Creative Jobs AI Enables
Healthcare	Data entry, basic diagnostics, administrative work	AI-assisted diagnostics, personalized treatment planning, AI system management
Manufacturing	Assembly line work, inventory tracking, quality checks	AI maintenance, robotics programming, system optimization
Transportation	Driving, route planning, scheduling	AI-driven logistics management, fleet optimization, customer experience improvement
Retail	Checkout, inventory management, customer service (basic)	E-commerce strategy, personalized customer experiences, AI-driven sales analysis
Administrative	Scheduling, data entry, document processing	Workflow automation design, digital transformation management
Finance	Fraud detection, data processing, compliance monitoring	AI strategy development, financial advising based on AI insights, risk management
Agriculture	Crop monitoring, irrigation control, routine inspections	Precision agriculture planning, AI-powered crop analysis, sustainability management

AI's Impact on Industry Transformation: From Repetitive Tasks to Higher-Level Jobs

But is AI killing jobs wholesale, or is it simply shifting the nature of work?

Real-Life Example: Automation in Financial Services

Consider the financial services sector. Traditionally, tasks like loan approvals, credit scoring, and data entry were handled by clerical staff and analysts. Today, AI can analyse thousands of financial profiles in seconds and make decisions faster than a human ever could.

Does this mean fewer human jobs?

Yes and no.

While certain clerical roles may no longer exist, new opportunities have arisen. Human workers now focus on **more complex tasks,** such as creating personalized financial plans or managing client relationships. They use AI tools to gather insights, but it's still their expertise that turns those insights into meaningful advice for clients. In this sense, AI is **reshaping** jobs, not eliminating them entirely.

Jobs That Will Disappear—and Those That Will Thrive

Of course, some jobs will undoubtedly disappear as AI takes over routine and predictable tasks. Jobs that are repetitive and require little creativity or critical thinking are at risk. For instance:

- **Data entry clerks** have seen a decline, as automation software can handle massive amounts of information far more quickly and accurately.
- **Warehouse workers** are being replaced by AI-guided robots that can move inventory, pack boxes, and even prepare products for shipment.
- **Telemarketers and customer service agents** may find their roles reduced as AI chatbots and voice assistants improve.

But on the other hand, new careers are flourishing:

- **Data scientists, AI specialists, and automation engineers** are in high demand as organizations look for professionals to design, implement, and maintain these advanced systems.
- **Creative professions** like marketing strategists, graphic designers, and content creators are discovering new ways to collaborate with AI tools to enhance their creativity and productivity.
- **Healthcare professionals** such as doctors and nurses are leveraging AI to assist in diagnostics, but it's their judgment and human interaction that remain critical to patient care.

Real-Life Example: The Rise of AI Ethicists

As AI becomes more prevalent, **AI ethics** is emerging as a crucial field. Companies and governments are realizing that AI systems must be monitored for bias, fairness, and transparency. This has created an entirely new career path: **AI ethicists**. These professionals ensure that the algorithms guiding AI decisions do so in a way that's fair and just, free from bias or unintended consequences.

So while some traditional jobs may shrink, others—like AI ethics—are being created from scratch. And these are high-value roles that require a blend of technical knowledge and moral judgment, something that machines can't replicate.

A Partnership between AI and Humans: Collaboration, Not Competition

Throughout this book, we've seen a common theme emerge: **AI works best when it complements human abilities**. Instead of thinking about AI as a competitor for jobs, we should consider it a partner—one that enhances human potential by automating the mundane and routine, and freeing people to focus on what they do best: thinking creatively, solving complex problems, and building relationships.

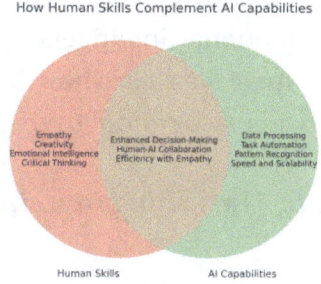

How Human Skills Complement AI Capabilities

Real-Life Example: AI in Healthcare

In healthcare, AI systems like **IBM Watson** can sift through vast amounts of medical data to suggest diagnoses or treatment plans. But it's still the doctor who makes the final call, considering not just the data but the **human elements** — the patient's emotional state, family history, and overall well-being. AI may be able to make the diagnosis faster, but only humans can provide the **empathy** and **personal insight** that comes with patient care.

This collaboration between human and machine is likely to be the model for most industries in the future.

The Future of Work: A Shift in Skills

The question is no longer whether AI will change work — it already has. The real question is: **How do we, as professionals, adapt?**

The answer lies in **reskilling** and **upskilling**. Workers need to focus on areas where humans excel, such as creativity, problem-solving, emotional intelligence, and leadership. At the same time, they must also learn how to work with AI tools, leveraging them to increase productivity and innovate.

Real-Life Example: Upskilling in Retail

The retail industry offers a glimpse into this future. With the rise of AI-driven sales platforms and automated checkouts, traditional cashier roles may shrink. But smart retailers are investing in **training programs** to help workers transition into roles such as **customer experience specialists**—people who can offer personalized advice, handle complex customer requests, and ensure smooth shopping experiences. These are areas where human intuition and emotional intelligence still hold a distinct advantage over machines.

The Human Factor: Why Jobs Aren't Going Away Anytime Soon

No matter how advanced AI becomes, certain elements of the human experience will always remain outside the reach of machines. **Empathy, creativity, and complex problem-solving** are areas where humans thrive, and where AI still struggles.

Machines may be able to process data at incredible speeds, but they lack the ability to understand **nuance, emotion**, or **context** in the way that humans do. This is why, despite fears of job loss, there will always be a need for human workers in **education, healthcare, creative industries**, and other areas where personal interaction and critical thinking are essential.

Will AI Kill Our Jobs?

So, will AI kill our jobs? **Not exactly.**

The reality is that **AI will change jobs**, but it won't eliminate them. Certain roles will disappear, and new ones will take their place. The key to thriving in this new world is adaptability—embracing lifelong learning, mastering AI tools, and focusing on uniquely human skills that machines cannot replicate.

AI isn't here to replace us. It's here to **empower us**, to help us work smarter, faster, and more creatively. The future of work isn't about competing with machines—it's about **collaborating with them**.

The professionals who recognize this and adapt to the changes will be the ones who succeed in this evolving landscape.

AI and the Future of Work: Reinvention, Not Elimination

End View:

As we reflect on the question that has guided this book — *Will AI kill our jobs?* — the answer becomes clear: AI will not kill jobs; it will **transform them**. The fears surrounding AI and automation are understandable, but history has shown us time and again that while technology may shift the landscape of work, it also creates new opportunities.

In this new era, **adaptability** is key. The future workforce will be a blend of human creativity, empathy, and leadership, complemented by AI's speed, precision, and data processing capabilities. As professionals, the path forward is not to fear AI, but to **embrace it**, harness its potential, and focus on the areas where humans excel.

For those who are willing to learn, evolve, and collaborate with technology, the future holds boundless opportunities. The journey of AI in the workplace is just beginning, and those who see it as a partner, rather than a competitor, will not only survive but thrive.

In the end, AI won't kill our jobs — it will **redefine** them, helping us unlock **new possibilities** in the world of work that we have yet to fully imagine.

AI Energizes the Workforce: Amplifying Human Potential

Introduction:

Imagine a world where professionals in every industry have access to a personal assistant—one that never sleeps, can process vast amounts of data in seconds, and provides valuable insights to make better decisions. This assistant isn't human—it's AI. And rather than taking over jobs, AI is **energizing professionals**, empowering them to excel in ways previously unimaginable.

But how exactly does AI amplify human potential? How is it becoming a tool that enhances productivity, creativity, and efficiency? And most importantly, how does AI allow professionals to focus on the tasks that truly matter? This chapter dives into how AI is not just reshaping industries but **energizing professionals** across sectors by making them more effective, informed, and innovative.

AI as the Ultimate Support Tool

AI isn't replacing professionals—it's providing them with tools to **supercharge their capabilities**. The real power of AI lies in its ability to process information at speeds and volumes that no human could match, giving professionals the chance to focus on more creative, high-level work. Whether it's assisting with routine tasks, analysing data, or providing real-time insights, AI becomes the partner that makes professionals more effective in their roles.

Take, for example, the field of **engineering**. AI tools are helping engineers simulate complex designs, analyse data from prototypes, and predict failures before they happen. This saves time, reduces costs, and allows engineers to focus on innovation and problem-solving rather than getting bogged down by repetitive calculations.

Case Study: AI in Healthcare

Nowhere is AI's energizing effect more apparent than in healthcare. Doctors, nurses, and medical professionals are increasingly turning to AI tools that enhance their ability to deliver care. **AI-powered diagnostic tools** can analyse medical images or patient data at incredible speeds, allowing healthcare providers to make faster, more accurate decisions. This means doctors spend less time on paperwork and data analysis and more time focusing on their patients.

But this isn't just about efficiency — it's about **elevating care**. AI tools can spot patterns and anomalies in data that might go unnoticed, providing healthcare professionals with a deeper level of insight that helps improve patient outcomes. In this sense, AI energizes the healthcare workforce by helping them provide better, more informed care to their patients.

AI: A Creative Companion for Professionals

Contrary to the myth that AI lacks creativity, we're seeing how AI is actually **boosting creativity** in industries like **marketing, design, and content creation**. AI can generate ideas, analyse audience data, and automate repetitive tasks, freeing up creative professionals to focus on the strategic and emotional aspects of their work—the parts that require human intuition and imagination.

In content creation, AI tools like **Jasper.ai** *are helping writers brainstorm ideas or generate drafts, but it's still the human touch that gives those stories heart and creativity*

For example, **AI in marketing** can analyse market trends, customer behaviour, and ad performance, offering data-driven insights that inform creative campaigns. Marketers still drive the creative vision, but AI helps them make smarter, faster decisions about what will resonate with their audience. In this way, AI doesn't replace creative professionals; it enhances their **creative decision-making**.

Energizing the Supply Chain: From Logistics to Retail

AI's ability to streamline operations is energizing professionals in sectors like **logistics, manufacturing, and retail**. **AI-powered supply chain management** tools help professionals forecast demand, optimize inventory levels, and identify the most efficient shipping routes. What used to be manual processes prone to human error are now optimized through AI, making supply chains faster, more flexible, and more reliable.

In retail, AI assists with everything from **automated checkouts** to personalized shopping experiences, allowing sales professionals to focus on more meaningful interactions with customers. Retail workers are no longer just clerks—they're becoming **brand ambassadors**, focusing on customer service while AI handles the more transactional aspects.

AI as a Professional Development Catalyst

AI is also playing a significant role in **professional development**. From **personalized learning platforms** to **upskilling programs**, AI is transforming how professionals learn and grow. Platforms like **Coursera** and **Udacity** use AI to recommend courses based on individual learning styles and career goals, helping professionals continuously update their skills in real-time.

Also, Platforms like Coursera and edX offer certifications in AI-related fields, and many of these programs are free or low-cost, making it accessible to anyone looking to upskill.

In this way, AI isn't just a tool for professionals to use at work—it's becoming a partner in **lifelong learning**. By making education more accessible, tailored, and engaging, AI is ensuring that today's workforce remains competitive in tomorrow's world.

Real-Life Example: AI in Hospitality and Tourism

The **hospitality and tourism** industry is undergoing a transformation as AI begins to enhance how professionals deliver customer experiences. AI chatbots are being used to handle customer inquiries, assist with bookings, and provide personalized travel recommendations. This allows hotel staff and travel agents to focus on creating exceptional guest experiences.

For example, in luxury hotels, AI-driven systems can predict guest preferences, automate check-in processes, and manage room service requests—all without sacrificing the human touch that defines hospitality. By handling these logistical tasks, AI enables hospitality professionals to dedicate more time to interacting with guests, offering the **personalized experiences** that keep customers coming back.

In **tourism**, AI tools can optimize travel itineraries, assist with language translation, and provide travellers with real-time information about flights and accommodations. This helps travel professionals focus on more value-added services, such as crafting unique experiences or handling complex travel requests.

Preparing for the AI-Driven Future

To fully harness the power of AI, professionals need to embrace **collaboration with machines**. This means learning to work alongside AI tools, not as competitors but as **partners** that can amplify human strengths. As AI takes over the more routine and data-driven aspects of work, professionals are free to focus on higher-level tasks—whether that's strategic decision-making, creative problem-solving, or fostering human connections in customer-facing roles.

The essential skills for the future will be a mix of **technical proficiency**—to understand and leverage AI effectively—and **human skills** like communication, empathy, and creativity that AI cannot replicate.

According to a McKinsey report, nearly 14% of the global workforce will need to switch jobs or acquire new skills by 2030 as a result of AI and automation.

Conclusion: AI and the Empowered Workforce

In the end, AI is not here to replace us; it's here to **empower** us. Across industries, AI is giving professionals the tools they need to excel in their roles, taking care of the routine tasks that slow us down and providing insights that help us make smarter decisions. The question is no longer, "Will AI kill our jobs?"—it's "How can we **work with AI** to reach new heights?"

In the coming years, the most successful professionals will be those who see AI not as a threat, but as an opportunity to **amplify their potential**, unlock **new levels of creativity**, and tackle challenges that we've only just begun to imagine.

Together, humans and AI will shape the future of work in ways that are exciting, innovative, and transformative.

Throughout every revolution, AI has always supported human growth. The fear that AI will take away our jobs is not a reality. In all industrial revolutions, people have feared that new technologies would eliminate jobs, but history shows this isn't true. Instead, these advancements have consistently created more jobs than they replaced.

Conclusion: The Future of Work – Humans and AI, Partners in Progress

As we reach the end of this exploration, one truth stands out: **AI is not here to kill our jobs**, but rather to **transform and redefine** them. Throughout the chapters of this book, we've travelled from the birth of computing and automation to the rise of AI, discovering along the way how technology has continuously reshaped the workforce. While AI is a powerful force, its true potential lies not in replacing human workers, but in **augmenting human capabilities**.

In the early days of computing, there were fears that machines like ENIAC would make human labour obsolete. These concerns echoed through the decades as new technologies emerged—robots on assembly lines, personal computers in offices, and now AI systems capable of performing tasks that once required human intelligence. The fear has always been the same: Will we lose our jobs to machines?

A New Perspective: AI as a Tool for Empowerment

However, history has shown us that technology doesn't simply destroy jobs—it changes them. The introduction of **ATMs** didn't wipe out bank tellers; it allowed them to shift from routine transactions to more complex customer service roles. The rise of **word processors** didn't eliminate typists; it

Conclusion: The Future of Work – Humans and AI, Partners in Progress

opened up opportunities for workers to develop new skills and take on higher-value tasks.

Similarly, **AI is set to transform the nature of work** across every industry, from healthcare and education to manufacturing and hospitality. AI will handle the repetitive, data-driven tasks, but the **human element**—our creativity, empathy, and judgment—remains irreplaceable. We've seen AI assist surgeons in operating rooms, help farmers make data-driven decisions, and enhance customer service in hospitality. Each example illustrates a critical point: AI is a tool, and like any tool, its value lies in how we use it.

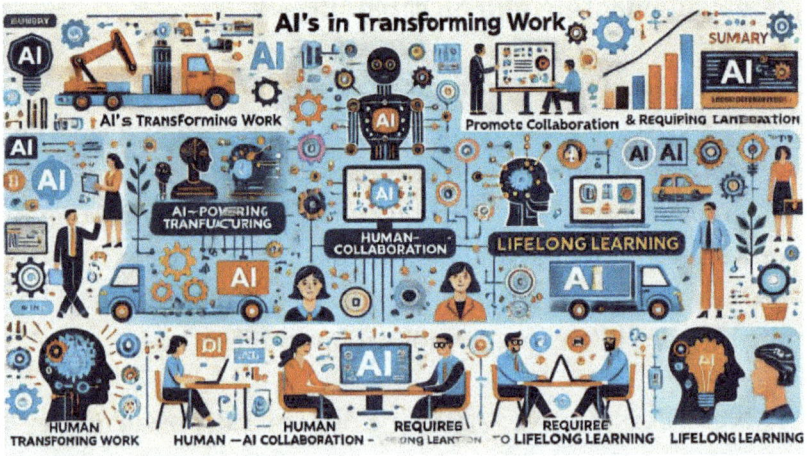

AI's Role in Work, Collaboration, and Upskilling Summary

The Collaboration between Humans and AI

The central theme of this book is the idea of **collaboration between humans and AI**. AI can handle data at speeds and scales that are impossible for humans, but it still relies on us to provide context, insight, and a guiding hand. This collaboration is the key to the future of work—a future where machines handle the mundane, leaving humans free to focus on the creative, strategic, and interpersonal aspects of their jobs.

The professionals who will thrive in this new landscape are those who learn to **embrace AI as a partner**, not a threat. AI will help engineers design more efficiently, healthcare workers diagnose with greater accuracy, and supply chain managers optimize complex systems. But it is still human intuition, creativity, and decision-making that will drive progress.

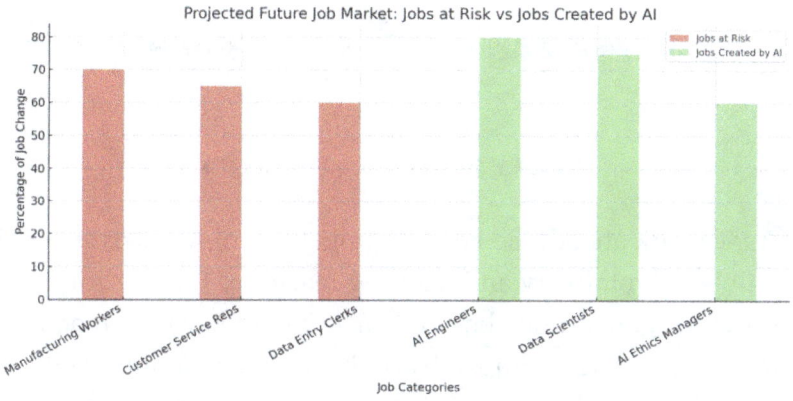

Projected Future Job Market: Jobs at Risk vs Jobs Created by AI.

Preparing for the AI-Driven Future

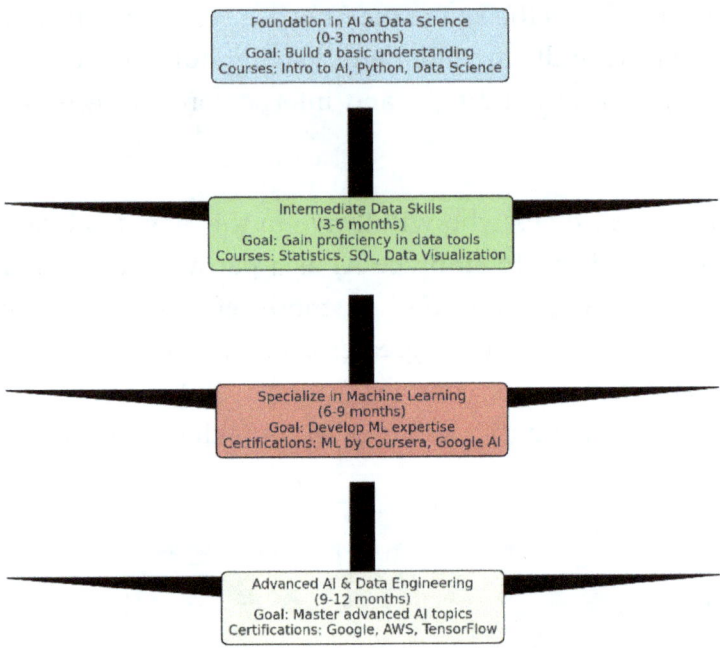

AI and Data Science Learning Path Flow Diagram

As we look ahead, the key to navigating this AI-driven world will be **adaptability** and **lifelong learning**. Just as workers in previous generations had to learn how to use new machines, today's workforce must learn how to collaborate with AI systems. Upskilling, reskilling, and continuous education will be critical. Governments, businesses, and educational institutions must play their part in ensuring that workers are prepared for the shifts that AI will bring.

It's essential to recognize that while some jobs will be displaced, new roles will emerge. In fact, many of the fastest-growing jobs today — **data scientists, AI ethicists, automation engineers** — are a direct result of advances in AI. The workforce of the future will need to combine technical skills with the **human skills** that AI cannot replicate — critical thinking, communication, and creativity.

AI and the Human-Centred Future

Ultimately, AI should be seen as a **force for empowerment**, not displacement. When trained and implemented properly, AI will enable us to tackle challenges we once thought impossible, from advancing medical research to solving global supply chain issues. As we continue to develop AI systems, the focus must remain on creating a future where technology **amplifies human potential**.

A report from the World Economic Forum predicts that while AI could displace 85 million jobs by 2025, it will also create 97 million new ones, particularly in data analysis, AI development, and green energy sectors.

So, will AI kill our jobs? The answer, as we've seen, is **no** — not if we rise to the challenge. AI is transforming the workplace, but with that transformation comes opportunities for growth, innovation, and collaboration. The workforce of tomorrow will look different, but it will be built on the same foundation: humans, working together, empowered by technology.

In the end, AI will not define the future of work—we will. By embracing this new era with curiosity, adaptability, and an open mind, we can ensure that the future of work is not one of loss, but one of limitless potential.

Acknowledgment

Writing *Will AI Kill Our Jobs?* Has been a journey filled with exploration, reflection, and discovery, and this book would not have been possible without the support and guidance of several incredible individuals.

First and foremost, I want to extend my deepest gratitude to the experts and professionals across various industries who generously shared their insights and experiences. Your knowledge and contributions have been invaluable in shaping the ideas and real-world examples presented in this book.

To my friends and family, thank you for your unwavering support, encouragement, and patience. Your belief in this project sustained me during the long hours of research and writing. You inspired me to dig deeper, think critically, and always stay focused on the broader vision of the book.

I would also like to thank the educators and mentors who have influenced my understanding of both technology and the workforce. Your teachings and perspectives helped guide the development of the central themes in this book.

Finally, a heartfelt thanks to the readers who picked up this book with curiosity and an open mind. I hope it has provided you with valuable insights and sparked thoughtful reflection on the future of work in the age of AI. This is a conversation that is just beginning, and I'm grateful to have you as part of it.

Postscript

As we reach the end of *Will AI Kill Our Jobs?* the question posed at the outset remains a complex one. The world is entering an era where the impact of AI will be felt in every industry and profession. However, as we've explored in these pages, AI is not merely a force of destruction or creation; it is a tool — one that holds immense potential to either empower or disrupt, depending on how we choose to harness it.

This book is not intended to offer definitive answers but to provoke thought and dialogue. The future of work is still being written, and its narrative will be shaped by our actions today. Whether AI will replace jobs or create new opportunities depends on how we, as individuals, businesses, and societies, adapt and respond to the challenges and opportunities ahead.

As you turn the final page, I encourage you to remain engaged with the evolving conversation about AI and the future of work. Stay curious, continue learning, and always consider the human role in shaping the technologies that shape us.

Remember, the future is not something that happens to us — it's something we create. AI won't determine our destiny; we will. Let's ensure that our collaboration with technology paves the way for a future where both innovation and humanity thrive side by side.

Thank you for being part of this journey. The conversation continues.

Once again thank you for reading this book.

Let me know your thoughts: gowthamsamys@gmail.com

www.ingramcontent.com/pod-product-compliance
Lightning Source LLC
Chambersburg PA
CBHW050257230526
45471CB00005B/1919